Member
Hints & Projects

Handyman Club of America

Minneapolis, Minnesota

Member Hints & Projects

Credits

Mike Vail
Vice President, Products & Business Development

Mark Johanson
Book Products Development Manager
Handyman Club of America

Jay McNaughton
Book Marketing Coordinator

Bill Nelson
Art Director and Production

Gina Seeling
Art Director and Production

Greg Pluth
Photo Production and Photography

Kim Bailey
Photography

Cover Photo
In-progress woodcarving in butternut created by Tom Devaney of St. Louis Park, Minnesota. Photo by Kim Bailey.

ISBN O-914-697-91-9

Handyman Club of America
12301 Whitewater Drive
Minnetonka, Minnesota 55343

Foreword

This is a book written by and for the members of the Handyman Club of America. We asked our Club Members to share the tips, hints, projects and problem solvers they value the most. What you'll find on the following pages are the best of the many enthusiastic replies we received. These clever and resourceful ideas have not been published in any previous Club publications. I think you'll find them to be unique, helpful, and above all, extremely interesting.

In this new book you'll find helpful hints of four general types: handyman hints for the do-it-yourselfer in all of us; hints for the workshop; woodworking hints that could save you some time and money on your next project; and home and yard tips that will help you keep your property looking its finest.

In the Member Projects section you'll see a gallery of finished projects completed by your fellow Club Members.

It's a vast array of furniture, accessories, backyard building, storage solutions, remodeling projects and full-scale building projects—all undertaken by members of the Handyman Club of America. It would be hard to page through this colorful section and not find some inspiration for a project of your own.

I hope you enjoy the ideas, the creativity, the practicality and the many photographs our Members have contributed to make this book a reality. And if this book gets you excited to finish a project you've started, or to launch a brand new project you hadn't ever thought of before, then don't forget to take a picture or two when you're done. You may get another chance to see your own work featured in a Club book soon—and at *American How-To* we're always happy to review your submissions for Tip Trader or HandyWorks in our magazine's Club News section.

Tom Sweeney

Tom Sweeney
Executive Director
Handyman Club of America

Table of Contents

Member Hints

Member Projects

Member Hints

Being a Handyman is a lifelong learning process. Each new task we confront and every project we accomplish teaches us something: a new technique, a cheaper alternative, a way to save time... It's from these lessons that our skills and our confidence grow. But being a Handyman is not just about learning. It's also about teaching. For the shortcuts we discover and the improvements we make are worth very little if we keep them to ourselves. And more than that, sharing our successes and passing on our ideas to others is one of the most gratifying benefits of our pursuit. On the following pages, many Club Members have taken the time and effort to share their own bits of wisdom and experience with the rest of us. They have become teachers in a field that has no limit to what can be learned.

HANDYMAN HINTS

A crowning achievement

Once while listening to a neighbor complain about how difficult a time he had trying to install some crown molding in his dining room because he couldn't find the wall studs easily, I thought there must be an easier way. In fact, a way that only one person would be able to start and finish a project without a second pair of hands.

I went into my shop with a piece of molding that I wanted to install in my home, and measured the distance between the molding and a corner of the wall it would cover. I created a wedge by bevel-ripping a 2 × 4 on my table saw. Then I cut the wedge into small sections and installed them at the junction where the ceiling meets the wall. Here, it is clearly easier to nail the wedge into the top plate without fear of missing a stud.

After the wedges were installed, it was time for the molding to be installed. It is a more simple job now to install the molding directly to the wedges—so simple only one person can do the whole job.

Mike Brescia
Doylestown, Pennsylvania

Wedges made by bevel-ripping a 2 × 4 are nailed to the top plate of the wall, creating sturdy nailing surfaces for a tricky crown molding installation.

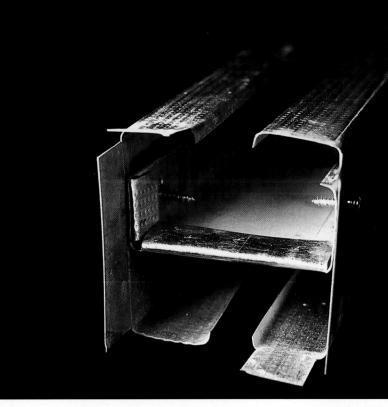

Inserted at a right angle to two metal studs, an interior stud greatly increases the strength and rigidity of a metal corner post or door jamb.

"I-beam" stud takes the flex out of metal posts and jambs

With the increasing use of light gauge metal studs in commercial as well as residential construction, one might find that doors just don't sit as solidly as with wood construction.

For the cost of one additional stud, the builder can turn a typical flimsy box jamb into an I-beam. By simply putting a single stud 90° between the typical box detail, a once semi-rigid jamb will become rock hard.

Nick Hastings
Newberg, Oregon

Note from the Club:

METAL STUDS: *While most of us are more accustomed to working with all-wood framing members, metal studs are growing in popularity. Although they can be a little harder to use than a plain old 2 × 4, metal studs offer a few advantages: they're lightweight and easy to transport; they're fire resistant; they're relatively inexpensive; and they're less likely to bow, warp or suffer movement than wood studs. And by inserting blocking (like a scrap of wood 2 × 4) near a cutting line, you can eliminate one of the biggest complaints about metal studs: that they twist, bend and vibrate when they're cut.*

This ceramic wall tile drill was fashioned from a piece of steel tubing and a steel washer—the washer does the cutting.

The hole for this water supply pipe was cut using Phil's home-made tile drilling tool.

Drilling tool for ceramic wall tile

I invented an idea for drilling holes in ceramic wall tile. I used a steel tube section which was nothing more than a piece of shaft tubing from a discarded golf umbrella. I split the tube with a hacksaw to create a slot in one end, then inserted a sturdy steel washer into the slot. I crimped the washer in place by flattening the end of the tube with a ball peen hammer. I chucked the other end of the tube into my drill press. The abrasiveness of the washer is enough to remove the tile material as I lower the drill press quill, and once I've broken through the surface the round washer cuts a perfectly smooth hole for pipes or other obstructions.

Phil Duck
Columbia, South Carolina

Binding the backs of parquet tiles with duct tape prevents separation caused by the vibrations of a jig saw. Be sure to remove all the duct tape and any adhesive residue before you glue the tiles down.

A better way to cut parquet

When installing wood parquet flooring, and cuts are needed along walls or around doorways, place strips of duct tape on the back surfaces of the floor tiles prior to cutting. The tape will help hold the wood pattern together during jig-saw cutting by preventing the 12 × 12 in. parquet tiles from separating.

This is especially convenient with prefinished floor tiles consisting of 4 × 4 in. squares bound into 12 × 12 in. tiles. The duct tape can then be easily removed to ensure proper adhesion of the tile with the subfloor.

Randy J. Hedgeland
Columbia, Maryland

Quick cure for cracked tiles

I'm a ceramic floor tile layer and every now and then I have to go back and replace damaged, cracked or loosened tiles. Instead of mixing a batch of Thin-set *mortar for just one tile, I find that using* Liquid Nail *adhesive (the subfloor type) is as effective, without having any leftovers.*

All I do is spread an even coat on both the floor surface and the back of the new tile, set the tile, and Presto! Instant repair, without cleaning buckets or a trowel. Then just let the adhesive set for a day and apply grout as you normally would.

Samuel Saribay
Lahaina, Hawaii

Rub-a-dub-dub, try mixing concrete in your tub

Mixing concrete by hand is hard, messy work. I used to use a wheelbarrow or a mortar box, which hold only one or two 60-pound bags, and don't offer very good access for turning the mixture.

A year or two ago I remodeled my bathroom and took out the old plastic bathtub. I knew that to install the new pressed steel tub correctly, I should set it into a mortar bed for leveling. I didn't want to bring my wheelbarrow upstairs to mix just two bags of mortar, so I emptied the *Thin-set* dry mix into the old bathtub, added some water, and stirred it up with a flat-nosed spade. The long, shallow tub gave me plenty of arm room for mixing, and when I was done, I just took the old tub outdoors, tipped up the foot end, and rinsed the leftover mortar right out the drain hole!

Now I keep the old tub stowed in the garage, and I use it for all my concrete or mortar mixing projects (I make sure to prop up the drain end first, though, so the water doesn't run out while I'm mixing). And if my neighbors look at me funny, I just tell them I'm installing a hot tub for my deck!

Bud Burma
Bangor, Maine

The neighbors might chuckle a little to see him, but Bud swears by his practice of mixing concrete in an old bathtub. He simply props up the drain end on some blocking, then turns the mixture with a spade. When he's finished, he washes out the residue through the drain hole. And because it's plastic, the old tub is easy to transport and store.

A hack saw blade can be used to create a new slot in a stripped screw head. Because of the tight quarters, you'll find it easier to get at the screw head if you remove the blade from the saw—be sure to wrap the end of the blade to protect your hand.

Cut a new slot to set stripped screws free

A rounded-off, stripped screw head in metal or even wood or plastic can be a real headache. First, try setting the screwdriver head with a light hammer tap. If that doesn't work, use a hack saw blade and cut an indentation deep and wide enough to accept a standard flat screwdriver. The extra leverage will usually allow the added twist needed to set the screw free.

John D. Wood
Lawrenceville, Georgia

Before cutting a threaded rod or bolt, slip a nut up above the cutting line. Then unscrew the nut after making the cut to remove filings and clean up the threads.

De-burr bolts and threaded rods with a nut after cutting

If you need to cut a threaded rod or bolt, first screw on a nut past the cut-off point. Then when you finish cutting off the rod or bolt, back the nut off over the end of the bolt. The nut will straighten the threads after it passes over them. If the nut sticks, or if you meet resistance, tap the bolt, nut side down, on a hard surface. This will help straighten the threads that are deformed slightly. This trick often saves you from having to clamp the bolt in a vise or pliers to remove the nut.

John Probst
Huntersville, North Carolina

Insulate attic openings

I have designed a very helpful, energy-saving device which I installed to seal the attic entrance of my pull-down stairs.

THE PROBLEM: Commercially available pull-down stair kits installed for entrances to attic areas have no insulation and are not sealed. The result is winter heat loss into unheated attic space and summer heat infiltration into the cooled living space below

THE SOLUTION: Insulate and seal the pull-down attic stairs.

To do this, I built a wooden frame around the top of the stair opening. This frame incorporated a channel in which a rigid, high R-rated insulated board slides on a plastic "V" weatherstripping seal on the bottom of the channel. I attached a standard window pull to the insulating board. To the attic floor behind the opening I attached a board for the insulation board to slide onto. Then I installed a light switch in the side of the frame at the top of the stairs.

The insulating board I used is 2 in. thick with an "R" value of 14.4. The door could use a 4 in. thick board or receive another 2 in. board for higher "R" value. The insulating board should be faced with foil on the top side to reflect heat back into the attic.

James R. Tichenor
Buena Vista, Virginia

A layer of rigid insulation board fits into a track above the attic access opening to help prevent heat loss from an uninsulated pull-down attic door.

Lubricate glass before you cut

When you cut window glass with a glass cutter, a good trick to make sure the glass doesn't break is to wipe down the cutting line with turpentine before you make the cut. The turpentine lubricates the glass so the cutting head travels more easily and isn't as likely to skip around (which can result in a jagged cut or even cause the piece of glass to shatter when you snap it).

You can use other lubricants, like dish soap, to get the same result. But I like turpentine because it evaporates quickly and doesn't leave any residue behind on the glass.

Phillip Partridge
Cheyenne, Wyoming

The adhesive backing on some materials, like acrylic or polycarbonate, often can be released using low heat from a hair dryer, making the backing easier to remove.

Low heat is a sure-fire way to release adhesive backing

When trying to remove old or damp protective coating from polycarbonate sheets, first heat the entire surface area with a hair dryer or similar device. Then you can peel off the entire side of backing. The extra time required to dry the paper will be far less than what would be required to peel off pieces of paper and rub off the adhesive.

Robert W. Manthey
Cannon Falls, Minnesota

Flashing in a flash

I have 22 years of experience as a carpenter. Ten years ago I had to flash a 120-foot deck attached to a house. The old method for bending flashing was taking a 2 × 4 to it and bending it into shape. I had an idea for a better way to do it.

To make a 90° bend, I make two "L"s from a 2 × 4, and lay one inside the other so the corners are together. I measure out along the inside corner of the outer "L" and mark points for the length of each side of the flashing (a good proportion for 12 in.-wide flashing is to have one side be 4½ in. and the other 7½ in.).

I put spacers between the "L"s, about the same thickness as the flashing. Then I drive nails at the measured points to keep the flashing on track. I attach the unit to a solid structure, then score a centerline partway down the flashing with a utility knife. I bend the scored end to a 90° angle, then feed it into the space between the "L"s on the unit, and push it through to the other side. Then I pull the flashing through the gap, guided by the nails (it helps to have a second man feeding the rolled flashing through to prevent binding or buckling). The result is a uniform bend that is the desired length and very rigid.

By cutting the corners of the 2 × 4 s to other angles , you can bend flashing for other jobs (like a roof valley).

B. Falvey
Westboro, Massachusetts

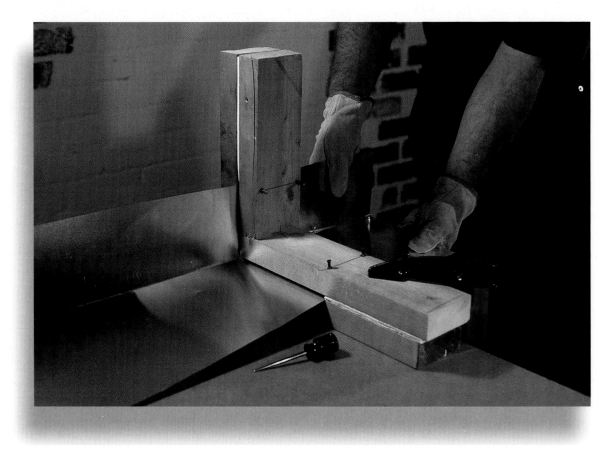

This device for bending flashing works a little bit like an extruder, with the rolled flashing fed through the gap between the L-sections.

The heat from a small engine muffler that's been running for a while is about the right temperature and intensity for softening plastic pipe to make it pliable.

Note from the Club:

PRECAUTIONS: *Ed's tip can be used successfully with just about any vehicle or tool that has a combustion engine (like the lawn mower shown in the photo above). But be sure to use good sense and avoid touching the exhaust system, and if the process don't be tempted to apply the pipe directly to the muffler—you could damage your equipment. Also, do not use this technique for bending water supply or drain pipe—the heat will weaken the area where the bend occurs. Instead, use flexible tubing or the appropriate plastic pipe connectors and fittings.*

Bending pipe in the field

While installing PVC pipe out in the country, I needed to make some offsets and bends in the plastic conduit. Looking for a way to heat the pipe, I noticed a garden tractor sitting nearby. I started the engine and let it warm up for a few minutes. Then I held the plastic pipe an inch or so away from the muffler. In no time at all, the pipe became pliable enough to make the bends and offsets I needed.

Since then I've used this method often. I find that I don't get the scorch marks that may result when using a propane torch or some other type of open flame to heat the pipe. Naturally, it's important to rotate the pipe during the heating process in order to ensure uniform pliability. It is also important to check for pliability quickly, as it does not take long with this method.

Ed Haberl
Fort Atkinson, Wisconsin

Attached to an old hose and filled with water, these plastic bottles work as a height leveling tool for checking the relative height of two different spots. When the bottles are at the same height, the water levels will be precisely equal.

Doing its level best

I discovered a great idea for using a discarded 75-ft. garden hose. I simply took two small 20-ounce plastic soft drink bottles and drilled a 9/16 in. hole in the bottom of each bottle with a spade drill bit. Then I connected one end of the hose to the throat of each bottle. I now have a water level gauge that I can use for checking brick foundations, setting fence posts, etc.

Through the holes in the bottoms of the bottles, add enough water to the assembly to fill the hose and partially fill both bottles. Tie or strap one bottle at one end of a straight run, then position the other bottle at the other end of the run. Adjust the second bottle up and down. When the water levels are exactly the same in both bottles, the heights will be even.

Phil Duck
Columbia, South Carolina

All-plywood door vise

I made a simple and lightweight door vise to hold doors steady while you work on them. The whole thing is made of ¾ in. plywood. The vertical supports are spaced 1⅞ in. apart to accommodate standard exterior and interior doors. The bottom piece is set up on two ½ in. plywood "feet" to provide sideways stability and to allow the bottom to flex from the weight of the door, which tends to bind the door at the top. It isn't necessary for the door to be held rigidly and you only need one of these door vises to hold a door. I put a screw eye on top to hang it from the rafters when not is use.

Robert Fleming
Santa Ana, California

The coarse nap on commercial carpet is abrasive enough to sand drywall joint compound. Dip the carpet in water first to keep dust to a minimum.

Wall-to-wall joint compound sander

If you are bothered by the dust created by sanding drywall joints after taping, try sanding with a flat scrap of commercial carpet dipped in water. Rinse the carpet piece often in a pail of water. Allow ample time for the wall to dry before painting.

Dick L. Hinesley
Tecumseh, Oklahoma

The inside edge of the nose plate extension for this hand truck is notched with keyhole notches, fitting over the frame of the hand truck (Right).

When not in use, the extension plate can be lifted up and out of the way, and attached to a rubber band on the hand truck frame (Below).

Nose plate extension makes hand truck more versatile

An over-sized nose plate for a two-wheeler hand truck is convenient when unwieldy items like large garbage cans need to be moved around on a stable platform.

You can create a suitable enlargement for your needs with ¾ in. plywood or high-density particleboard. My hand truck is constructed out of 1-in.dia. steel tubing and features steel wheel fenders. These fenders could be added to a hand truck if they aren't present.

The tube frame measures 12½ in. wide, and the nose plate measures 8¾ × 13¾ in. The extension piece I cut from particleboard is 13 × 16¾ in.

To install the extension piece, I laid out center lines to align with the frame tube. From the edge of the platform, I marked a center point in ¾ in. for the tube holes to be cut. Next, I made a saw cut from the edge of the platform into each side of each hole to create a "keyhole" effect. The width of the "keyhole slot" is slightly larger than 1 in. to more easily insert the platform enlargement squarely onto the existing nose plate and under the fenders. Even if your load is very heavy and the platform rises upward, the fenders keep the platform in place.

Next, I placed a single drywall screw into the leading edge of the plate and can store it on-board by means of a rubber band looped around the center of the frame tube.

Basil G. Petimezas
Johnstown, Pennsylvania

The search for the perfect plug has been going on practically since caulk cartridges were invented. Using wire connectors to seal off the top of the nozzle is one solution that has shown some promise.

A new use for an everyday item

I tried different methods to plug the top of partially used caulk or adhesive tubes to prevent them from drying out. All of them failed. Then I tried using a wire connector, and it worked!

Because the inside of the wire connector is threaded, it screws on easily and securely. You can use different size connectors, depending on how far down from the tip the tube nozzle has been cut. And if you're like me, you've got plenty of the little connectors floating around in your tool box.

Jalil Hakim
Houston, Texas

Get rid of styrofoam packing materials, and add a useful project accessory in the process. Burlap bags or rice bags filled with packing peanuts make light, comfortable kneeling pads for working on hard surfaces around the house.

Make knee pads for peanuts

Here's a way to deal with those pesky styrofoam packing peanuts. Simply fill an empty 25 pound or 50 pound reinforced plastic rice sack (or a burlap bag) with the peanuts, leaving enough room at the open end to fold over twice. Then, using an ordinary office stapler (or a needle and heavy thread) seal the open end shut. Now, whenever you need to work on cement or any hard surface on your knees, use the peanut bag as a knee cushion.

I have found that you can actually drop onto this cushion knees-first from a standing position without any shock whatsoever. When the styrofoam eventually crushes down and starts to crumble, open the bag and refill it with fresh styrofoam.

Peter S. Birnbaum
Sebastopol, California

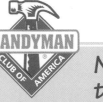

Note from the Club:

PEANUT IDENTIFICATION: *This tip is a nice idea for actual styrofoam peanuts (if you can't find rice bags, check your local coffee shop for empty burlap coffee bags). But these days, it's becoming more common to see corn starch-based peanuts used as packing material (they're much more environmentally friendly). The problem is that the corn-starch peanuts will disintegrate if they become damp, which makes disposal easy but would cause a real mess inside a rice bag. To test the peanuts, just dab a little water on them. If nothing happens, they're probably styrofoam.*

Whipping a chain through sand or pebbles will eventually remove rust—plus it's a good way to release stress. Be sure to wear eye protection and pay close attention to make sure no one gets in your way.

Chain reaction removes rust

To remove rust from an old metal chain, whip it roughly through some sand, gravel or similar aggregate. The rust will disappear.

Dorothy Jahnke
Monticello, Minnesota

Note from the Club:

REMOVING RUST: *Here are two more tried-and-true hints for getting rid of rust:*

Naval Jelly: *This auto body shop staple neutralizes and clears up rust without damaging the metal. Apply it with a brush, then wipe clean with an abrasive pad.*

Carbonated cola: *To remove rust from a piece of hardware, drop it in a jar of carbonated cola beverage and let it soak for an hour or two. This method has been known to work, but isn't guaranteed.*

Poly rope spliced into loop makes handy cord hanger

A loop made from polypropolene rope is a great help in storing other ropes, hoses or cords (or anything that is stored coiled up). I have made several loops of varying dimensions to suit particular applications. The best loops are those with no knots, which you can make by splicing the ends of a length of poly rope together. There is a special tool called a *fid* that's basically a bullet-shaped thimble used to make a seamless end splice.

After coiling a length of hose, rope, or electrical cord you can simply wrap the poly cord loop around the coil, then back through the loop itself, and hang the other end of the loop from a hook. The heavier the coiled object, the tighter the loop carrier will hold.

Basil G. Petimezas
Johnstown, Pennsylvania

Polypropolene cord is a good choice for making loops because the ends can be spliced together (no knots needed) using a special tool called a fid.

A loop holds cords very securely when hung from a hook because it becomes more secure as the load increases.

Member Profile:

Phil Duck *Throughout this section, and throughout this book, you'll encounter the name* Phil Duck *on many occasions. An incredibly prolific generator of helpful hints and fascinating projects, Phil has a clever solution for just about any situation or challenge you can imagine.*

A resident of Columbia, South Carolina, Phil works in retail sales and has a budding computer networking business he operates from his home. When he's not dreaming up creative ideas and building better mousetraps, Phil spends time with his local church group and tries to keep tabs on his busy family (from Phil's descriptions, it sounds like inventiveness is definitely a family trait).

Thanks for all the great ideas, Phil—you're a perfect example of true Handyman spirit!

Phil Duck
Handyman Club of America

Convenient clamp holder

I constantly have a need for spring clamps when I'm working with my scroll saw. I discovered the perfect solution for keeping them close at hand: attach a bathroom towel rack with offset brackets to my tool stand to hold the spring clamps.

Phil Duck
Columbia, South Carolina

Custom-made blocks fit worksurface to a "T"

I use 2 × 4 T-blocks to protect my work surface from accidental scraping or cutting by the jig saw.

Phil Duck
Columbia, South Carolina

These 2 × 4 T-blocks have dowels on the underside so they'll fit into the bench dog holes on workbenches (both portable and stationary).

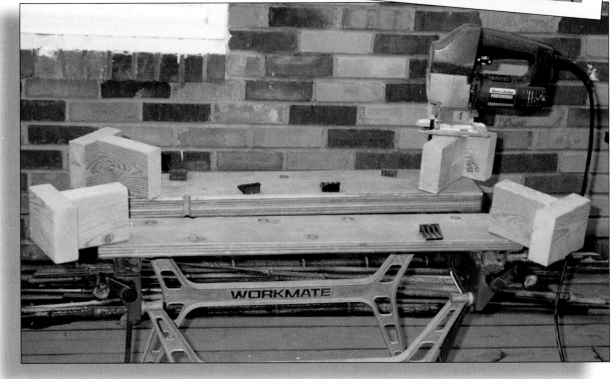

The T-blocks can be adjusted to lift the workpiece high enough that a saw blade can't damage the worksurface.

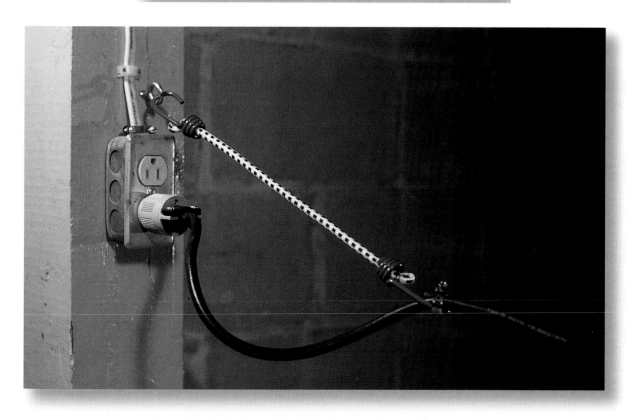

Secure extension cords with a rubber strap or bungee cord near the outlet to keep them from coming unplugged.

Give extension cords a brake

To keep an extension cord from coming unplugged, take a rubber strap (bungee cord) and affix one end to your extension cord on the male end. Be sure to tie off the extension cord so the part on the outlet side is about 10 in. longer than the length of the rubber strap. Take an eye bolt about 2 in. long and install it above your plug, to the left or right side about ¾ in. off center. Be sure not to screw the eye bolt into your power supplying wire.

Thomas B. Case
Duckhill, Mississippi

A shot of everyday oven cleaner and a stiff brush will remove most resin build-up from the teeth and gullets of your saw blades. Be sure to wear rubber gloves when using oven cleaner.

Oven cleaner cuts blade resin

This tip saves you money as well as wear on your circular-saw blades caused by being sharpened too many times—especially the carbide tipped ones.

Most of the time when your saw does not cut properly, it's not because the blade needs sharpening. It's because the saw is running hot and burns the boards you are cutting. This is caused by resin build-up on the teeth and in the chip gullet. Therefore, the blade usually needs cleaning, not sharpening.

I spray oven cleaner on the teeth of both sides of the blade, let it set for two or three minutes, then use a wire brush to scrub the resin off the blade. Then I wash the blade off well with water and examine it. I sometimes have to spray it again, depending on how much resin has built up on the blade. When the blade is clean, I dry it off thoroughly with a paper towel or rag, and immediately apply a liberal coat of oil or *WD-40* because the blade will start to rust quickly. The clean blade will cut like a new one.

Safety warning: Be sure to use rubber gloves when working with oven cleaner because it contains sodium hydroxide. If you're working in an enclosed area, also wear a respirator mask.

Earl H. Kellam, Sr.
Huntsville, Alabama

The narrower tube in this home-made assembly adjusts up and down on the shank of the drill bit to set exact drilling depth when using a portable drill.

Portable drill stop

Once I needed a series of consistent-depth holes for a workpiece too large for my drill press. I came up with this idea. I combined a ½ in. drill bit, a drilled-through rubber stopper, a ¾ in. coupling (which fit snugly over my drill chuck) and a piece of ¾ in. dia. PVC pipe.

A rubber stopper fits into one end of the narrower, ¾ in. dia. tube. After the drill bit is chucked, the coupling is fitted over the stopper, tube and drill chuck.

The shank of the drill bit fits into the rubber stopper, and also serves as a stop for the narrower piece of tubing. As you move the stopper and narrow tube up and down on the bit shank, the drilling depth changes. The coupling fits over the tube, stopper and chuck to keep everything aligned.

Phil Duck
Columbia, South Carolina

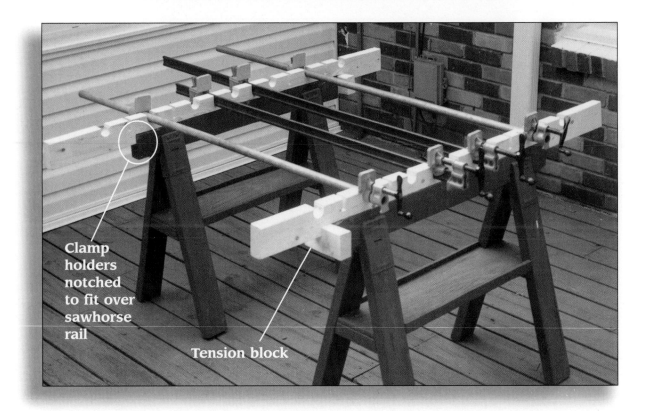

Clamp holders notched to fit over sawhorse rail

Tension block

These 2 × 4 clamp holders are designed for clamping panels and other wide glue-up projects. The notches in the tops of the holders are sized to accept either pipe clamps or bar clamps, with the clamp heads positioned on the outsides of the holders. The undersides of the holders feature notches the same length as the saw horse rails, so the holders can fit snugly over the tops of the rails. Tension blocks, also made from 2 × 4s, are attached to the bottoms of the holders just inside the notch on one end. The tension they create helps keep the holders secure when they're fitted over the rails.

Saw horse accessory supports and aligns clamps for gluing panels

I designed and invented this "fishbone design" for converting common sawhorses into a clamping rack station. It features a unique tension block idea and is designed to accept either pipe clamps or bar clamps.

Phil Duck
Columbia, South Carolina

Framework platform adds versatility to ordinary saw horses

I designed this simple idea of cutting lap-joints in 2 × 4s so they'll fit together and fit on top of saw horses. When I first put one of these assemblies together, I thought I was designing a better way of supporting wood panels for rip-cutting. After jumping up and down on it, however, I discovered that by simply adding an intermediate 2 × 4, the structure could be used to support a scaffolding board. The lap-joint frame can be assembled in less than a minute.

Phil Duck
Columbia, South Carolina

Lap joints cut into the edges of these 2 × 4s serve a dual purpose: they allow the boards to fit together and to straddle saw horses. When used with sturdy saw horses, the assembly creates a broad, stable platform for supporting large workpieces, or even for supporting a scaffolding board—just make sure the feet of the sawhorses are level and secure before attempting to use the set-up for scaffolding.

Screwdriver tune-up can correct the effects of abuse

There's one tool in the workshop that gets used for many tasks besides the one it was created for: the screwdriver. It can serve as a chisel, a scratch awl, a hole punch, a pry bar, a can opener, a staple remover, or a paint stir stick . . . just to name a few. As a result, the screwdriver is probably the most abused tool in the shop. While it's a good tool for the above tasks and many others, it often fails at one simple task—driving screws.

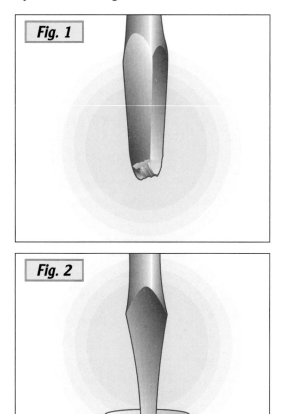

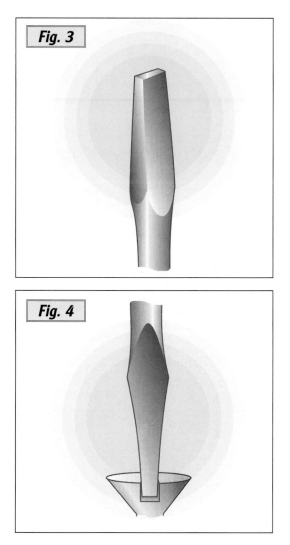

Figure 1 shows a worn screwdriver tip. **Figure 2** shows how a worn screw head fits in a screw slot. The only metal-to-metal contact is at a sharp angle, so when twisted the tip will push itself up and out of the slot. The user must apply a lot of downward pressure and more twisting force than should be necessary. Often the result is a stripped screw head and a gouge in the piece you're working on.

Figure 3 shows a new screwdriver tip. **Figure 4** shows how it fits in a screw slot. Note the amount of metal-to-metal contact and the near-square fit. All that is needed to drive the screw is a twisting force, with very little downward pressure.

Just about every home has an assortment of these wonderful "miracle tools" that could be used as screwdrivers if the tips were simply restored to a like-new condition. Fortunately, that isn't difficult. While screwdriver tips are hardened, they can be worked with a file and a grinding wheel.

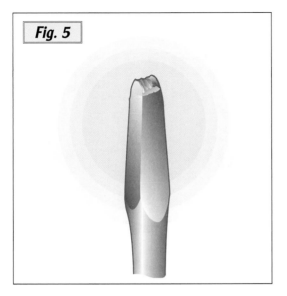

Fig. 5

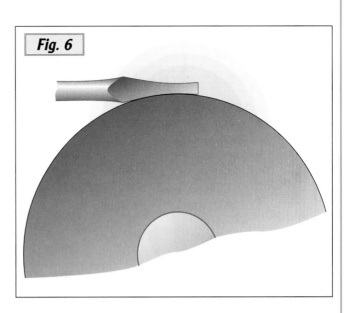

Fig. 6

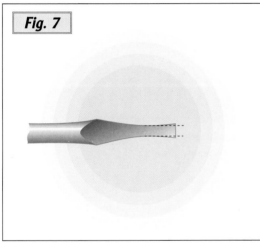

Fig. 7

The first step is to flatten the tip back beyond any rounded corners, as in **Figure 5.** You will then need to get rid of the sharp angle that forms at the tip of an abused screwdriver. This can be done by forming a "hollow grind" as in **Figure 6,** then hand filing the tip to make parallel lines at the very end, as in **Figure 7.** If you don't have a grinder, skip the hollow grind and start filing. It will just take a little longer this way. Make sure you keep the edges of the tips parallel to each other. If the edges are not parallel, they will form a wedge that will move sideways and out of the screw slot when pressure is applied.

Be careful not to make the tip too thin. The ideal thickness is one that will completely fill the screw slot on the screws you use most often. The tighter the tip fits in the slot, the more metal-to-metal contact you have and the less likely the driver is to slip out of the slot. You can regrind some of your other screwdrivers to fit a variety of screw sizes.

You can also custom grind the width of the tip to fit the screws you use exactly. Using a tip that is not as wide as the screw head requires more twisting force due to decreased leverage. Using a tip that is wider than the screw makes twisting easier, but you risk damaging the wood when you get close to the surface.

The first time you try to regrind a screwdriver tip it probably will take several tries to get the tip right, so be patient with yourself. With a little practice you'll be able to regrind a screwdriver tip in less than five minutes. Soon you'll find that driving screws is not as hard as it used to be. But don't get carried away and regrind all your screwdrivers—every shop needs at least one all-purpose "miracle tool."

Grant Beck
West Jordan, Utah

Mounted on the inside faces of drop-down cabinet doors, these benchtop power tools stow away quickly and easily. When they're needed, they can simply be lowered out of the cabinet to create an efficient work area.

Benchtop tool storage solutions:
Mount tools on drop-down cabinet doors

Being severely cramped for room in my mini-workshop and unable to lift my benchtop tools, I put the tools in a cabinet with drop-down doors. The overall measurements of the cabinet will vary according to the make and model of the tools—mine are mounted on a 36 in.- high cabinet with an overall length of 7 ft. 6 in. The height is 26½ in. and the depth is 16½ in.

Nails replace the hinge pins on the drop-down doors so the tools can be quickly and easily removed for portability. The miter saw and the router table are placed at the rear of the door, otherwise the door will not close. A second hinged section permits me to get closer to my work. Each tool can become a work area of its own, and they all store away neatly when not being used.

Richard G. Ernst
Phoenix, Arizona

By mounting all of his benchtop power tools on identical 10 × 18 in. pieces of plywood, Matt can set the tools up interchangeably on his everyday workshop surfaces.

Benchtop tool storage solutions:
Mount tools on plain plywood

My shop, which is in the back of my garage, is small. In order to maximize the area I have, I mounted each of my bench tools to a 10 × 18 in. piece of ¾ in. plywood. Then, when I need to use the tool, I mount the plywood to my bench. Each piece of plywood has an identical pattern so that the location of my bench tools is interchangeable, and I don't need to drill a lot of holes in my bench. This also allows me to use the tools on my *Workmate.* This system allows me to move the tools around, depending on the space I need for my project.

Matt Hawkins
Byron Center, Michigan

Two-by-four runners underneath these plywood tool bases make it easy to clamp tools to a worksurface, and they also simplify transportation.

Benchtop tool storage solutions:
Add 2 × 4 clamping rail to plywood base

I have a nice size shop, but it is as large as it can get right now. In order to have my two workbench areas (one is 3 × 7 ft. and one is 3 × 3½ ft.) available for any type and size of project, I have come up with the following solution for use with my benchtop power tools.

I have mounted all of my benchtop tools to ¾ in. floor underlayment. I also attach a piece of 2 × 4 the same width as the plywood to the underside of each plywood panel. So far I have mounted my router table, bench grinder, small drill press, and disc/belt sander this way. I also have a spare "table" with various mounting holes in it for when I borrow other power tools, such as my father's scroll saw.

To use my benchtop tools I have a portable workbench. The "tool table" sits on the workbench and is clamped down securely by the 2 × 4 on the bottom.

To store my tools I have installed 2 × 3 or 2 × 4 rails under my workbenches with a piece of ¼ in. hardboard fastened to each one. The "tool tables" slide onto these rails, with the bottom 2 × 4 guided in the middle and the hardboard giving clearance from the cross members. This solution has been very handy and beneficial to me. Now my benchtops are unobstructed, except for one bench vise.

William Grosse
Yardville, New Jersey

Theodore Dudash gets the most out of his shop vac by attaching it to his woodworking machines through a simple network of tubes, connectors, and good old duct tape.

Shop vac is the heart of makeshift dust collection system

I used my wet-dry vac in the workshop all the time. So I thought "Why not use it to make a central dust removal system for my woodworking machines?"

I used flexible vacuum tubing and fittings, PVC fittings and central close-caps outlets. The outlets allow me to close off the suction on tools I'm not using. By installing a "T" connector on the main vacuum line, I'm able to attach my shop vac to more than one tool at once. And it disconnects easily when I need to use the vac for general cleaning.

Theodore Dudash
Crown Point, Indiana

Manufactured work lights can be expensive power tool accessories. Using a seat clamp for a bicycle post to attach an ordinary work light was a big money saver.

A bright idea for attaching work light

I came up with the idea of using a bicycle seat post clamp to anchor my flexible-arm spotlight lamp. I bolted it to the stationary arm of my scroll saw and inserted a small section of PVC pipe to secure it after I removed the lamp base. It saved a lot of money!

Phil Duck
Columbia, South Carolina

Carpet scraps make great shop aides

When we replaced the wall-to-wall carpeting in our living room last year, we were left with quite a pile of floor covering to dispose of. I didn't want to pay the disposal fee for bringing the whole mess to the waste processing center, so I started cutting it up into small sections and throwing the pieces away with my regular trash.

As I was kneeling on the carpeting and cutting it with my utility knife, it occurred to me that maybe the carpet and pad hadn't completely outlived their usefulness. I saved several strips of each, and now I use them for kneeling surfaces for projects all around the house and yard. And I also cut a few larger pieces to set beneath my workbench. Now when I drop a tool, it hits the carpet, not the concrete. And if I spill paint or oil (which I do sometimes) I can just get rid of whichever carpet piece it messes up. And one more advantage: my legs have never felt better after standing at my bench for a long time.

Richard Peterson
Patterson, New Jersey

Hose clamps strategically placed on the stress points can keep vacuum tubes from cracking.

An old wheel rim filled with concrete is the anchor for this do-it-yourself vise stand.

Well-placed reinforcement prolongs shop vac life

Twenty five years ago, I decided that I was going to get every nickel's worth out of my shop vacuum. I installed stainless steel hose clamps at every one of four stressed connections of my hose. It worked! After all these years, no cracks in the tubing.

Phil Duck
Columbia, South Carolina

Stand up for your vise

I spot-welded a 2-ft. section of 2 in.-dia. thick-walled galvanized pipe to an automobile wheel to create a mountable base for my machinist vise. I weighted it down by adding cement to the wheel. I then cut a heavy steel surface to mount the vise to. Next, I welded a flange that was threaded to accept a 6-in.-long section of pipe to fit inside the main pipe. It rotates 360°, is freestanding, and portable enough to move anywhere in my workshop.

Phil Duck
Columbia, South Carolina

Leather handle covers stitched together from an old hand bag make these tools more comfortable to work with.

For a better grip that's easier on the hands . . .

I enjoy leather craft. Twenty five years ago, I stitched leather over my hand tools. It really was a lot easier than it looks. I used a discarded ladies handbag to make the pieces. I suggest lubricating the handle with dish soap for fitting the covers on. Then, a simple twist should tighten the cover.

Phil Duck
Columbia, South Carolina

Cheap pre-filter for shop vacs

The paper filter cartridges in most brands of shop vacs have a tendency to clog with the fine dust created in sanding, particularly when there is any dampness. Even before the tank fills up, you can begin to experience a loss in suction. I investigated. When I removed the top of the vacuum, I found that the fins of the filter were clogged with fine sanding dust. While it's easy enough to shake it out if it's dry, the smallest amount of dampness will make it stick and cake up. I found I had to take a small stick and scrape the fins to free them from the clog.

To prevent the paper filter from clogging, I used a piece of foam air conditioner filter material as a pre-filter. I cut it to size to wrap around the canister, and fastened it at the top and bottom with large rubber bands (you could also use string). This prevented the build-up of dust in the fins without any appreciable loss in suction. Sooner or later even this material will have a build-up of dust, but it's a lot easier to just remove the foam, rinse it out with a hose, squeeze it dry and wrap it back around the cartridge.

This method has extended the life of the actual filter cartridge many, many times. In addition, the cost of the air conditioner filtering material is very low—a lot lower than the cost of replacing the cartridge itself.

T.F. McCarthy
Souderton, Pennsylvania

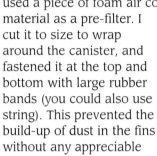

An everyday air filter for an air conditioner can be cut to fit over the paper filter cartridge on a shop vac. The easily-washable air conditioner filter will screen out most of the dust that can clog the regular filter.

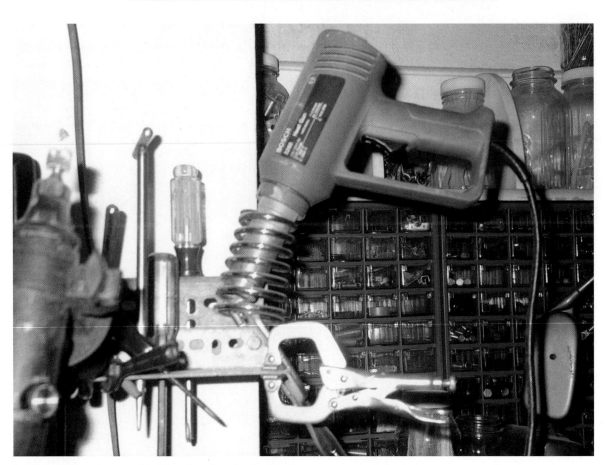

A heavy spring makes a cool holding place for a hot heat gun.

Hot springs?

I use a large spring from a local trophy shop to provide an unbeatable, handy tool rest for my heat gun. To suspend the spring at a comfortable angle, I use a pair of vise-grip-style "C" clamps. Now I don't accidentally burn myself.

Phil Duck
Columbia, South Carolina

Note from the Club:

HEAT GUN SAFETY: *Heat guns produce a high-volume flow of air at temperatures up to 1200°. It should go without saying that these tools require careful operation. There are many very safe applications for heat guns, but avoid using them to strip paint from woodwork in your home—particularly along the baseboards. The danger here is that the gun will actually cause paint chips to smolder, at the same time blowing them into the gap between the baseboard and the floor, where they can smolder for hours and potentially cause a fire inside the wall.*

Using either end of a box wrench, you can drive eyebolts and eyescrews easily and with minimal slippage.

A tip from a driving instructor

When driving in large hooks, eyebolts, and similar hardware, I would like to suggest an idea that works well for me. Just use a box wrench to drive them home—and to remove them as well. Try to maintain constant turning tension.

Phil Duck
Columbia, South Carolina

Swivel flange

Control ventilation in your shop by attaching a fan to the ceiling with a rubber strap and a swivel flange—the swivel shown here is from an old punching bag.

Fan and swivel are a one-two punch

I mounted a swivel flange from a punching bag to the ceiling of my basement workshop. I combined a simple loop over the handle of my fan with a rubber bungee, and I can now aim the fan in any direction to provide comfortable ventilation while I work.

Phil Duck
Columbia, South Carolina

First-aid for worksurface cuts

As my brother was ripping a 4 × 8 sheet of plywood on my portable workbench, he accidentally sawed a deep kerf through the plywood surface of the workbench.

To reverse this otherwise tragedy, I removed the 'culprit' circular saw blade and used it as a thickness gauge to cut a softwood shim on my table saw. I installed the shim in the kerf using epoxy, then planed the surface until it was even with the rest of the worksurface. Now I can forget that it ever happened at all.

Phil Duck
Columbia, South Carolina

Using the saw blade that scarred his portable workbench as a thickness guide, Phil cut a shim to match and epoxied it into the kerf created by the saw.

PVC tool holders store and protect awkward portable power tools

I cut 5½-in.-dia. PVC drain pipe sections to fit awkward electric power tools such as jig saws, drills, grinders etc. To anchor the pipes and to provide increased rigidity and strength, I rip-cut 3½-in.-wide strips of the pipe to the length of the PVC sections and install them inside the holders with corresponding matched holes to allow for carriage bolts. The slots in the holders can be custom-cut with a jig saw or hack saw to accommodate your power tools.

Phil Duck
Columbia, South Carolina

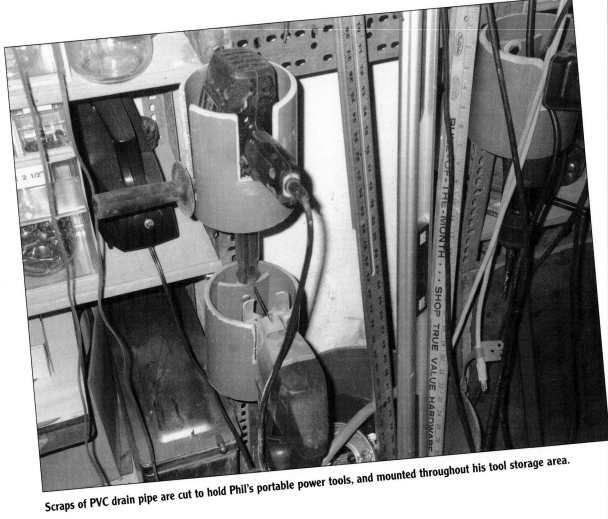

Scraps of PVC drain pipe are cut to hold Phil's portable power tools, and mounted throughout his tool storage area.

An adapter made from a rubber O-ring and shrink tubing helps an ordinary funnel work more efficiently

Funnel reducer

Many storage containers have openings that are too small to fill neatly, even with a funnel. The solution is to modify a funnel to make it fit the opening perfectly. Fit a snug-fitting rubber O-ring over the tip of the funnel, then place shrink tubing so it overlaps the O-ring about 3 in. Apply heat from a heat gun to create a seal with the funnel tip extension.

Phil Duck
Columbia, South Carolina

Grab onto a good idea

Before coming up with this idea, I agonized over finding a suitable handle to withstand the demands of this 40-pound-plus loaded tool box. I transferred this pop-up handle from a discarded *Samsonite* suitcase by drilling matching holes in each end. I think I'll paint it yellow.

Phil Duck
Columbia, South Carolina

Note from the Club:

TOOL STORAGE: *It's no secret that one of the greatest enemies of tools is rust. That's why a lot of professional mechanics keep their tools in waterproof storage containers. If you live in a humid climate and have a few tools you're especially fond of, try storing them in an insulated cooler. For extra protection, add a layer of sawdust at the bottom to absorb moisture. Lay a few pieces of scrap wood in the sawdust to prevent contact with the tools.*

Using the outward pressure of one spring clamp to force the jaws of another spring clamp together will boost your clamping power.

Double your clamping power

I discovered a way of greatly increasing the clamping capacity of my quick-grip hand clamps. Spring pressure is about double when used in tandem, mated in this reverse fashion.

Phil Duck
Columbia, South Carolina

WOODWORKING HINTS

Perpendicular clamping system

I've invented a way of holding wood planks at 90° angles.

I enjoy building doll houses and miniature house. I've found the smaller the room, the greater the demands for absolute accuracy and precision. For 90° clamping blocks I band-saw cherry chevron shapes and square them with a disk sander. I use Japanese miniature brass bar clamps to hold the floors and walls square to one another as the glue sets.

Phil Duck
Columbia, South Carolina

This creative clamping system is used to clamp two perpendicular boards when doing miniature work. A full-scale version can be used to clamp perpendicular panels.

Ninety-degree clamping blocks are cut from cherry and sanded square with a disk sander. Also shown are two Japanese miniature brass bar clamps that are clamped to the clamping blocks from each direction.

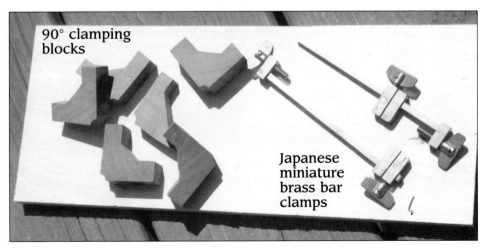

90° clamping blocks

Japanese miniature brass bar clamps

Surgical tubing retains its energy when wrapped tight, making it an excellent product for clamping irregular shapes. It can be purchased at most larger drug stores.

A grip like a boa constrictor

The simplest suggestions are often the best. I have one. I've read dozens of suggestions on how to clamp things while glue dries. The more irregular the shapes and angles, the more of a project it becomes.

The best answer I've found is surgical tubing. I purchase it in lengths of 12 ft., in both ¼ in. and ⁵⁄₁₆ in. outside diameter. To use it, you merely wrap it around and around, stretching it to add tension, then tuck in the end under the wrap. It adds plenty of pressure for gluing and will take care of the sharpest angles and the roundest or most irregular surfaces with ease. It doesn't slip, even on odd shapes.

Richard Frye
Clio, Michigan

Sanding secrets:

Perfectly proportioned sanding block:
Even though I have several different power sanders, there still seem to be times when a bit of hand sanding is needed. I found there is an optimum-size sanding block that is easy to handle and makes effective use of regular sized sandpaper sheets.

I cut a piece of ¾ in. thick wood to 2¼ in. × 4½ in. I use a quarter-sheet of sandpaper folded in half across the narrow dimension. One end is then folded up around the 2¼ in. width of the sanding block. This gives you enough sandpaper to grip. When that part of the sandpaper is exhausted, I fold the other half of the quarter-sheet around the sanding block.

The dimensions of this sanding block are perfect, Robert Fleming says, because it is easily controlled and it makes very efficient use of sandpaper.

Sandpaper cutter: Not finding the sandpaper grit I want in half-sheet or quarter-sheet size is no longer a problem for me. Rather than trying to cut it freehand, I made a simple sandpaper cutting board from a scrap of ¼ in. plywood, slightly oversize. I marked the 9 × 11 in. outline, and then made half-way marks in each direction. As an added touch, I included a pair of stop blocks in each direction.

To cut the sandpaper, I lay it on the outline, grit-side down. Following the guidelines, I use a utility knife and metal straight edge to cut the sheet to the size I want.

Robert Fleming
Santa Ana, California

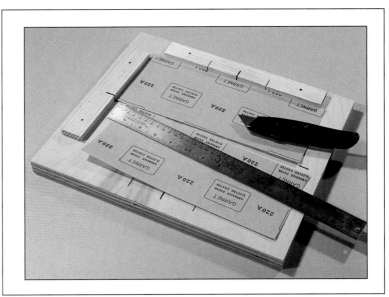

This sandpaper cutting tool is essentially a template with permanent alignment stops. The cutting is done with a utility knife and straightedge.

Mounted to a sturdy wooden box, this miter saw can travel easily and features room for storing your back saw and accessories below.

Miter box with integral storage

I invented this box as a storage helper for my hand miter saw. I first cut the "doughnut holes" at each end to provide balanced portability. Then I cut a fitted slot at each end of the box for the saw. Then I dovetailed my corners and attached the miter box to the box.

Phil Duck
Columbia, South Carolina

A spoonful of filler makes the evaporation slow down

I like to use solvent-based fillers because of their fast drying times. Instead of continually sticking your filling tool into the can, quickly scoop out a suitable portion with a teaspoon. Then replace the lid just firmly enough to contain the solvent vapors and to allow it to be reopened with a slight pry from your filling tool.

Now take the spoonful of filler to the points to be filled and just slide it from the spoon with your tool. Remember to close the can firmly at the end of the job.

By using the spoon, you will not only retain more of the solvent in the can and prevent early drying, but you will find that you don't drop and waste the filler transporting it on your filling tool.

John A. Chisholm
Clawson, Michigan

Veneer guard

When working with a delicate veneered wood surface, I attach a felt-covered guard rail over the rails of my saw horses to prevent marring.

Phil Duck
Columbia, South Carolina

Note from the Club:

VENEERED PLYWOOD: *Veneered plywood is becoming an increasingly popular woodworking material, due mostly to the scarcity and expense of hardwoods. Red oak, maple and birch veneer plywood are available in many building centers and in most lumber yards. As the popularity of this material has grown, so has the selection. It's now possible to get plywood with cherry, walnut, aromatic cedar, ash, white oak and even teak veneer, to name a few. Common thicknesses include 1/8, 1/4, 1/2 and 3/4 in. The majority is rotary cut veneer, like you'll find on most fir or pine plywood, with its familiar bookmatch pattern—but you may be able to find some sheet goods with plain sawn or even quarter-sawn veneer. These types bear a greater resemblance to solid wood.*

In this simple workshop jig, the permanently attached guide boards are set at a precise 90° angle to eliminate any chance of errors when two workpieces are clamped to the jig tight against the inside corner.

Frame assembling box can't miss

I have designed a frame assembling box. The mitered frame pieces are inserted into the assembly box and clamped to secure them for drilling and fastening. A frame leveler (a remote T-shaped support) merely keeps the boards the same height while making the assembly. The boards (that form the "L" on the top of the box) are set with a framing square to allow the miters o fit perfectly.

Robert D. Leslie
Kittanning, Pennsylvania

Editor's Note: *Robert was kind enough to send a nicely finished prototype of his device for us to try out at Club headquarters. For making perfect frame corners, it can't miss. We had very good luck testing it out, as each joint we made came out to exactly 90°. Thanks for your participation, Robert. We're sure it will inspire some other creative thinkers in the Club to come up with their own designs.*

Robert Leslie displays his clever design for a frame assembling box.

Drill press hold-down

I prefer this homemade clamping method over any of my locking toggle or pneumatic clamping devices. I use mini-channel tracks in my drill press table and grind my carriage bolts to fit in.

Phil Duck
Columbia, South Carolina

Upside down drilling

I find small dowels extremely useful when I can drill small holes in the ends for toy axles. To ensure consistent results, I chuck wood dowels into my drill press and turn holes over a stationary, mounted drill bit.

Phil Duck
Columbia, South Carolina

If you can't wait to oscillate . . .

My tip is for a very low-tech oscillating, drill press drum sander, that works great. It can be put together in minutes, from material on hand in most shops.

I tied one end of a length of rope to the drill press handle, then wound it two turns counter-clockwise around the handle spindles. Then I laced it through a hole in my dust collector box and attached a short length of light chain for easy length adjustment. The chain is looped through a stirrup that I make with a piece of ¼ in. all-thread rod to minimize slipping on my shoe sole.

To make the drum sander oscillate, just rock your foot down continuously, letting the spindle return take the sander back up. It can be hooked up quickly any time, and can be used standing up for short projects.

Richard Gostomski
Owen, Wisconsin

A foot pedal connected to the spindle lever on the drill press is used to create up-and-down "oscillating" action on a drum sander attachment.

A tool that's been around for centuries, the turnbuckle, is still your best bet for breaking glue joints, Phil contends.

Breaking glue joints is nothing new

I cannot understand what all the excitement is over glue spreaders (reverse glue clamps). I have used this idea for most of my life—a simple turnbuckle to push glue joints apart. It also has the advantage of working as a main drive when used with 2 × 2 stock.

Phil Duck
Columbia, South Carolina

A very attractive idea

When varnishing a finished project, I found the following helpful: In between coats of varnish, I use a double "0" piece of steel wool to smooth the surface. Then I take a heavy magnet, place it on a sheet of paper toweling, and pass it over the varnished area. This leaves any steel wool bits that are left behind clinging to the paper towel, and they are easily disposed of.

Don R. Jalbert
Miami, Florida

Editor's Note: *This tip is especially useful when using a water-based finish that can cause steel wool strands to rust.*

HOME & YARD HINTS

An occasional shot of hot water and bleach in the drain opening of your furnace humidifier helps keep the drain from clogging and causing a back-up.

Use bleach to keep overflow drains open

I have a preventative maintenance suggestion for those who have a humidifier hooked up to a hot-air furnace. The humidifier can back up and spill water down the side of the furnace. The water can't flow out through the drain pipe because it is plugged up with gunk and scum.

Every four to five weeks, I pour a cup of hot water and a cup of bleach through the drain pipe of the humidifier to clean out the pipe. It not only cleans, but it also disinfects at the same time. You will be able to see the difference within a day.

Once you have established this process (say, after two months) all you have to do is mix ½ cup of hot water with ½ cup of bleach, and pour it into the drain pipe. This tip can also be used for the air conditioning units.

Bleach is an inexpensive cleaner and disinfectant, and can be used as often as you wish.

George P. Jesberger
Port Reading, New Jersey

Use wallpaper steamer as carpet seamer for minor repairs

I've discovered a good tip for repairing carpet thats glued to the subflooring (a full-bond carpet installation). If the carpet seam has loosened, causing tufts of carpet pile to unravel, steam the seam with a wallpaper steamer. The steam loosens the latex or glue enough that you can shift the carpet around at the seam to disguise the missing pile. Any of the inexpensive wallpaper steamers will work.

Roy F. Scherer
Garden Grove, California

Discarded wire cable spools have many uses around the house and shop, including serving as an organizer for your holiday lights.

A good way to wind up the holiday season

Never know what to do with those Christmas lights? It's always so hard to store them without getting them all tangled for next year. Well, I go to the local hardware store and grab some of the old electrical wire spools that they are going to throw away and take them home. Then I wrap the lights around the empty spools. This method of storing lights is much neater and easier than putting them in a box.

Shawn Brown
West Valley City, Utah

A simple dry well made of pea gravel can put an end to soil erosion at water runoff points and at gutter downspouts.

Pea-gravel dry well gives grass a chance

The main runoff from the drip channels of my house trailer had always caused very bad craters in the soil at the two down-sloped corners. I found a very simple solution. At the worst drip point, I dug a hole approximately 12 in. in diameter and 3 ft. deep. Then I filled the hole with pea-gravel from a garden store. I am pleased to report that last year I had grass move into the eroded space for the first time.

Vincent M. Boreczky
Fennville, Michigan

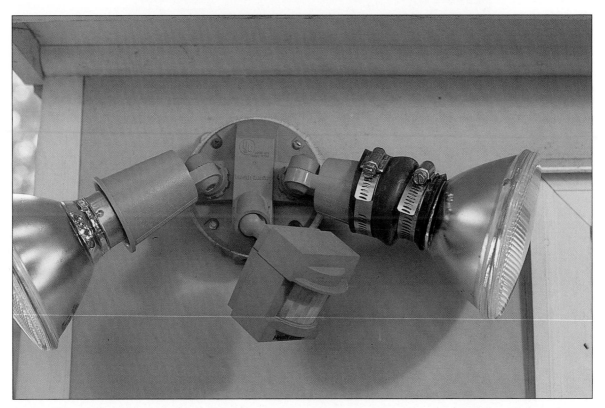

The flood light on the left can be removed easily in a second or two. The one on the right, secured with hose clamps and a strip of rubber, would require more effort to remove than many would-be intruders are willing to expend.

Secure your security light

Motion detector lights near your home entry are a good deterrent to intruders, but one drawback is that they can be disarmed in a few seconds by simply unscrewing the light bulb. This happened to me when my home was broken into recently.

To help make the the light more effective in the future, I screwed the new bulb in good and tight, then wrapped a strip of rubber around the area where the bulb meets the fixture.

Then, I tightened a 2 in. hose clamp at each end of the rubber joint—one is tightened around the base of the bulb, and the other around the end of the lampholder. Now, if someone wants to disarm the light, they've either got to unscrew a hose clamp or break the bulb. In the first case, they'll have to stand directly in the light for some time, and in the second case they'll have to make noise. I hope it's a pretty effective added deterrent.

Bud Burma
Bangor, Maine

Drill a hole through the stationary side of the hinge plate and into the fully inserted hinge pin. Then, insert a nail or wire of equal diameter into the hole to prevent the hinge pin from being pulled out easily.

Security tip: Pin your hinge pins

Here's a security tip. If you have a door in your home with the hinges on the outside, open the door and drill a hole in the non-moving part of the hinge. Drill all the way into the pin but not through the pin. Push a nail into the hole you have drilled, and cut the nail off with a chisel. Be sure to use your drill index or wire gauge to measure the nail first. It should not be too snug or too loose. This will help prevent a burglar from pulling the hinge pin out of the hinge.

Philip E. Keil, Sr.
San Antonio, Texas

New twist on an old favorite:
Use plastic newspaper bags for temporary storage of paint roller sleeves

Here's a time-saving tip. When you're doing a painting project and are done for the day, insert your brush and 7- or 9-in. roller and roller sleeve into one of those plastic bags newspapers are delivered in. The next day, they should be ready to use again. Roller sleeves and brushes can be kept this way for weeks. Roller trays can be put into tall kitchen trash bags.

H. F. Brown
Womelsdorf, Pennsylvania

Note from the Club:

Wrapping wet paint brushes in plastic has become a very popular practice—after all, who wouldn't jump at the chance to avoid a round or two of brush clean-up between coats? But for many of us, roller sleeves pose more of a challenge. They're too big for a sandwich bag, and wrapping them in plastic wrap can cause a real mess. That's why we liked H.F.'s tip so well: what a great use for those pesky little bags! One pointer: when you're done with the bags, turn them inside out and let them dry out on some newspaper before disposing of them (and don't forget to dry out your empty paint cans as well).

P.S. The newspaper bags work great for brushes too.

A little trick for preventing a big mess

When painting base-boards in carpeted areas, I found a way keep the paint off of the carpeting. I use old plastic venetian blind slats, slipping them between the base-board and the carpet. The curved side of the slat should be facing up.

Joan M. Janes
Savannah, Georgia

More handy hints for handling paint...

AN OUNCE OF PREVENTION: I have a simple remedy for keeping my arms and hands clean when I use a roller to paint ceilings. I wear my old knee length socks. It may look a little silly, but it works great.

Dennis Desormter
North Palm Beach, Florida

A POUND OF CURE: Seems everyone has a trick for cleaning oily hands, and most of them don't work. But here's one that I've had sure-fire success with. It's a two stage process: first, rinse your hands with a capful of vegetable oil (I prefer peanut oil), like you're washing them. This will dissolve the oily stains, as most people know. But it leaves your hands a slippery mess, so you're not much better off. That's where the second stage comes in: dishwashing liquid is great for cutting grease, so just rinse your oily hands with warm water and dish soap.

Jerry Jukbochowicz
Oak Park, Illinois

The light-duty wooden slides on wicker and rattan drawers can cause plenty of frustration. One Club Member addressed the problem by replacing them with new metal drawer slides.

Finally, a cure for sagging wicker and rattan drawers

The wicker three-drawer dressers we purchased some 20 years ago began to show wear. One drawer which had held a lot of clothing started to droop when pulled out. The problem? The ⅜ in. wooden side rails nailed to the drawer frame had splintered or broken off, allowing the extended drawer to droop.

I installed 16 in. steel side slide rails with roller-bearings. First, I removed what was left of the wood slides. Then I routed a 1-in. wide channel in each side of the drawer, on the outside, opposite the position where the wood slides had been. I routed to ⅛ in. depth in each ⅜-in. thick side. This allowed the steel rails to fit flush into the sides of the drawer. I chose 16 in. slide rails to fit 15 in.-deep drawers. The rail butts up to the drawer header.

Using ⅜-in. pan-head wood screws and construction adhesive, I mounted the standards to the dresser frame where the wood rail had been. I used a level and square to center the standards to the slides on the drawer, so the drawer would fit flush without scraping.

This new slide rail system improved the glide of the drawers. Not only was each drawer sliding more smoothly and easily, but we now have full access to the opened drawer.

Robert S. Kidd
Wichita, Kansas

Tidy paint cans minimize mess

Question: How do you keep a paint can lid free of paint while dipping your brush directly into the can?

Answer: Stretch two lengths of 2 in. wide tape across the open top of the can. The gap between the pieces of tape should be wide enough to allow your paint brush to pass

through easily. As you withdraw the brush, use the tape closer to the center to wipe off excess paint. The piece nearer the can will protect the lid from spills.

Phil Duck
Columbia, South Carolina

These slices of hickory, fitted with finish nails, provide extra support for hanging heavy items on the wall.

Picture perfect problem solver

Editor's Note: Finish nails or even special picture-hanging hardware are both fine for hanging ordinary paintings or photographs on your wall. But what about those heavier wall-mounted items, like mirrors or bookshelves? Even when you drive them into a wall stud, as you always should, they can bend or wear through picture-hanging wire. Phil's solution to the problem eliminates those potential disasters by distributing the weight of the item around the perimeter of the hickory chip (hickory is one of the hardest North American woods).

These easy-to-make "Picture Frame" wall hangers were cut from hickory chips at a 45° angle, using an 85-tooth carbide-tip blade mounted in a chop saw. I cut them about ¼ in. thick, then predrilled them for finish nails. They provide an incredible amount of weight support.

Phil Duck
Columbia, South Carolina

First, tie a loose, open knot in the end of the string. Then, wrap the string once around the bundle, double over the string, and feed it through the knot. Tighten the knot to hold the string in place.

It might seem loopy, but it's knot...

This tip is about how much string to cut off when tying a bundle of papers or magazines. Put a small knot in the string and wrap the string around the papers, drawing the string tight. Then stop the string loop from loosening by pulling a string loop in the knot. Pull a long enough loop to wrap the other direction around the papers. Pull the string tight and pull the loop to secure the knot. You can then continue to wrap the string for as many times as you want, without having to cut the string before you are finished. No more loose pieces of string laying around!

Patrick Cassidy
Jamaica, New York

Next, feed the doubled end of the string through the knot to create a loop large enough to encircle the bundle. Pull on the feed end of the string until the string is taut all around. Secure the knot. Then you can cut the string to the exact length you need.

Old paint pad and pole make a lightweight scrubber

I am 81 years old, and was recently faced with the challenge of washing a painted drywall ceiling. As I get dizzy looking up and am not able to use a ladder, I tried using an ordinary sponge mop with a six-foot handle. Unfortunately, I found it too heavy to raise up to the ceiling. I also tried to buy a refill sponge to fit a lighter unit, but was unable to find one.

Solution? I cleaned up some old paint pads that I used instead of a paint brush a few years back, attached the paint pad handle to a six-foot pole, and was able to clean the ceiling. This method would also work well for cleaning windows.

If you use Trisodium phosphate (TSP) as your cleaning solution, I recommend a rectangular plastic container be used for the cleaning solution and for the rinse water. You should also wear protective gloves as TSP is very rough on the hands.

In order to prevent making a big mess, you can use a paint roller handle to squeeze out the excess cleaning solution after you dip the pad. You should have two paint pads: one for the cleaning solution, and one for the rinse water.

Rudolph Chernich
Hoyt Lakes, Minnesota

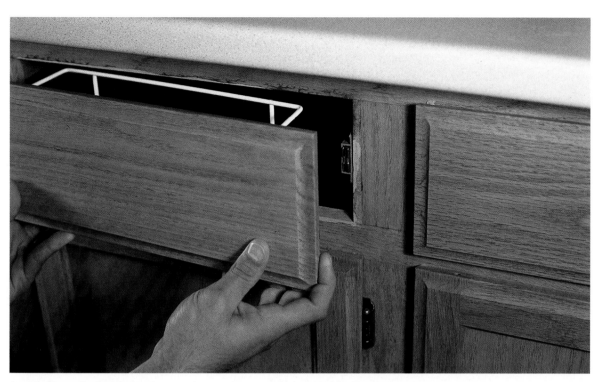

A magnetic catch placed at each corner is one way to convert a fixed false drawer front into a removable cover for your secret storage area.

False drawer front on sink cabinet can conceal secret storage compartment

I was looking for an inexpensive way to attach a false front to a sink cabinet. I tried to figure out a way to hinge it, but the only hinges that looked like they would work cost too much. So I used four magnetic catches instead. Once I got all four holding their own, it worked okay. The false front creates a hiding place for valuables.

Bill Gosnell
San Diego, California

> ***Editor's Note:*** *The space behind a false drawer face (usually found on cabinets beneath a kitchen sink) can make a great secret storage compartment. Once you've managed to remove the fixed drawer face, attach a small basket or box to the back side to hold the items you wish to keep out of sight. A lightweight silverware organizer, for example, will provide a generous amount of space for light valuables.*

Do-it-yourself shower rod...

I saved about ten dollars by making my own spring-loaded shower-curtain rod. I simply inserted a spring inside a section of ¾ in. dia. PVC pipe. To accomplish this, I force-fed a tube spring into one end of the tube, leaving ½ in. protruding. I added ¾ in. rubber end caps to each end.

Phil Duck
Columbia, South Carolina

...with a home-made shower curtain to match

Plastic drop cloths make terrific emergency shower curtains. Just staple a hem across one end and slide it over the shower curtain rod. Be sure the drop cloth is long enough to almost reach the bottom of the tub or shower pan. Because they're so lightweight, the force of the shower spray will make them balloon inward.

Joan M. Janes
Savannah, Georgia

Using the short end of the stick

I took a discarded, worn out yard rake and gave it new life. By simply shortening the handle and grinding the tips off flat, I now have a "wisp rake" to help scoop up leaves and straw.

Phil Duck
Columbia, South Carolina

When edging your lawn with a shovel, save yourself some back strain by using an alternating cutting pattern. In the diagram shown above, the best sequence would be 1, 3, 2, 5, 4, 7, 6. Each section equals one shovel width.

Getting the edge on edging

To help save your back when edging a lawn with a shovel, it is a good idea never to edge in a straight line. Instead I dig up every other segment by using a pattern of balanced resistance. To understand how important this is, insert a shovel to dig from a corner to a depth of about 6 in., then skip a space equal to the width of the shovel blade. Next, dig up the "in-between" section and continue on in this pattern. In other words, from your starting place dig the first section, then the third, then the second, then the fifth, the fourth, the seventh, the sixth, and so on. You'll soon be amazed at how effortless this becomes.

Phil Duck
Columbia, South Carolina

You may not find this use listed in the manufacturer's literature, but if you're looking for a way to save time and a little back strain when edging your lawn, you might want to try installing a coarse blade and using your reciprocating saw to do the job.

A reciprocating saw gets down & dirty

I have an unorthodox use for my trusty reciprocating saw. I attach a medium-length coarse (wood-cutting) or demolition blade to the reciprocating saw and use it to edge my lawn around sidewalks. The blade should be one you don't care much about, and the throat of the saw will plug up with grass and need to be cleaned, but it works and is cheaper than renting or buying a power edger.

To use the reciprocating saw as an edger, hold the saw so the blade is at about a 45° angle, and run the blade along the edge of the sidewalk.

Patrick J. Derosiers
Denver, Colorado

Truck mirror a good reflection on creative home security

My garage door faces the alley, away from the house. Because I have an electric garage door opener, I'm always concerned that I bumped the button on the remote control I carry with me on the way from the garage to my house. But because I can't see the door, I never know for sure unless I put on my boots and go out and have a look. After a while I got tired of doing this (my wife is one of those people who worries a lot about doors being closed).

One day a friend of mine parked his truck in the driveway, facing the alley, and I noticed I could see the garage door in his rear view mirror. Instant idea! That afternoon I went out to the auto salvage yard and bought an old truck mirror for next to nothing. I mounted it on the top corner of the garage, and now when I want to check the door I can see it just fine simply by looking out my back door.

Conrad Freebergh
Little Rock, Arkansas

A pair of clothespins provide a sturdy prop for keeping outlet covers open while you attach them.

Clothespins keep spring-loaded outlet covers at bay

Spring-loaded, weather-tight electrical outlet covers are nearly impossiblle to install by yourself, since the covers always close from the spring pressure, obscuring the retaining screw. By using two clothespins to prop open the cover, it's a snap to install these covers by yourself, regardless of the awkwardness of the location you may be working in.

Basil G. Petimezas
Johnstown, Pennsylvania

Gene Beck came up with a clever idea for saving money on his kitchen remodeling project. To make a new backsplash for the kitchen sink, he simply hung some textured wallpaper then coated it with six coats of polyurethane.

Built-up backsplash saved big money

When remodeling out kitchen we were faced with a dilemma: should we keep the ugly, 1970s fake tile pressboard backsplash, or should we rip it out and come up with an inexpensive replacement. We decided to rip it out.

I covered the drywall with ¼ in. lauan and primed it with wall size. Then we hung patterned, paintable wallpaper resembling an old pressed tin ceiling on the wall, and let it dry. Over the next three days we coated it with six coats of latex polyurethane. The polyurethane had the same effect as painting, as it defined the pattern of the wallpaper, while drying to a durable finish. It is washable and very easy to clean.

We applied a thin bead of silicone caulk to the base of the backsplash, then set plastic molding into the bead. The backsplash is into its third year and has given us no troubles. We are very happy with the results, and we saved a lot of money and labor compared to ceramic tile.

Tip: The wallpaper could be painted in various colors or patterns before applying the topcoat to change the effect.

Gene Beck
Brewer, Maine

A pair of salad scissors will make cleaning the gutters less of a chore when the Fall maintenance season comes around.

Get a grip on gutter clutter

I've discovered one of the best ways to clean leaves from my gutters. Just use common salad scissors, and you'll be amazed how much better they work than traditional plastic scoops.

Phil Duck
Columbia, South Carolina

Note from the Club:

Buying gutters: *Buying building materials or tools always requires some planning, but buying gutter materials can be especially misleading if you're not careful. Many building centers frequently run specials on gutters, especially the plastic ones. They'll advertise that their gutters are on sale for just a dollar or two per foot. That's all well and good, but if you're serious about purchasing new plastic gutters, keep in mind that most of the cost is not in the gutters, but in the hangers and fittings you'll need to install a gutter system. So to avoid any huge surprises at the checkout counter, bring a drawing of your house with you and carefully plot out the entire system, including all fittings, ends caps, hangers and downspouts. Then price the items and do some math. You may be surprised at the total.*

A fall from a ladder inspired Roy Lasko to devise a better, safer way to clean out his gutters. And now he even sells his inventon at local stores and craft shows.

A creative solution to a tiresome chore

Cleaning my eaves trough was a ladder-and-bucket operation. After falling from my ladder 2 years ago, I decided to make a tool I could use to clean the eaves trough from the ground. It required several modifications before I had a tool strong enough and with the right proportions to effectively clean my 100 feet of eaves trough within 15 minutes. Now I clean them more often with greater ease. I sell this tool through our local hardware store, and during craft shows.

Roy Lakso
Midland, Michigan

Member Projects

As Handymen, nothing excites our imaginations like the thought of a new project: a backyard gazebo, an attic conversion, a bookcase for the bedroom, or even something as simple as a new hand-made handle for a favorite old tool. And nothing fills us with more pride than seeing that project completed—that special moment after the last tool has been cleaned and put away and the last bag of construction waste has been carted off to the curb when we stand back and proudly admire our work. On the following pages you'll see dozens and dozens of projects, completed by fellow Club Members, that demonstrate quite clearly why we are what we are: Handymen.

FURNITURE PROJECTS

Wheelbarrow-style bench brightens garden setting

About five years ago my wife saw a wheelbarrow garden bench in a gardening magazine and wanted to have one someday. I made this bench for her last Christmas. It's my own design and required approximately 150 hours of labor. I am a carpenter/woodworker for a custom millwork shop.

The bench is made from river-recovered heart pine. The entire piece is completely done with joinery—no nails, screws or fasteners—and everything is glued with epoxy. The arm/leg pieces are each one solid piece, with the back supports bent at 15°. They are joined to the main rails with crosslap joints. The crestrail is joined to the back supports by mortise and loose tenon. The seat slats are doweled to the seat supports—not by drilling through but by predrilling the supports, then using spacers and dowel centers to mark the locations on each slat. The slats are attached with epoxy and dowels.

The arm slats are doweled as well. The tricky part is where the slats meet the back support. Each of the top five slats had to be cut at a different compound angle in respect to the angle and radius of the back support top. The backrest members and all remaining frame assembly were done with mortise and tenon joinery. After the bench was assembled I scraped it with a cabinet scraper, then applied an exterior finish.

The wheel is an actual wheelbarrow wheel that I bought from a local antique dealer. It's approximately 100 years old and is the exact size I needed. I repaired and painted the wheel as well as polished the solid brass collars at the ends of the axle. I think it adds a nice touch and its nice to know I'm reusing a piece of workmanship done by someone else long ago.

This bench is pretty darn comfy to sit in as we admire our hard work in the gardens.

David M. Rose
New Haven, Vermont

Pine hutch was custom-built right in the kitchen

My husband, David, made this hutch from solid pine, assembling it on-site in our kitchen. It measures 8 ft. tall by 8 ft. long. All the drawers operate using all wood drawer glides with no metal tracks. David built the hutch using his own design, without any purchased plans.

Sherry A. French
for David G. French Sr.
Tucson, Arizona

Member Profile:

David French Sr. *is a K-9 police officer for the city of Tucson, Arizona. He does woodworking as a hobby and for stress relief, says his wife, Sherry, who submitted several projects to the Club on David's behalf. "He deserves the recognition and I'm proud to give it to him," she added.*

CD rack a real space saver

This is the first real project I made with the *Shopsmith* I bought in the fall of '96. It came out quite well and it is very functional for the purpose for which I designed it.

My desire was for a CD rack that would hold as many CDs as possible in a small space. After a month or two of pondering (So, I'm slow!), I decided to make a six-sided wooden tube, with each side just wide enough to match the width of a CD. I spaced pegs up and down each side, and mounted the entire unit on a 12 in. Lazy Susan bearing. The unit is screwed to a heavy coffee table which also holds my stereo rack.

I fitted a cover to the top of the tube, and a shelf partway down inside the tube, to provide some storage. I cut the 60° angles for the sides and drilled them at a 15° angle for ¼ in. brass-rod pegs. Wood dowels would work as well and cost less. I left the pegs loose in their holes so they could be removed to allow for two-CD sets.

The height of the rack is dependent on how many discs you want to store. Mine is 39 in. high (tube only), and will hold 50 single discs per side, for a total of 300.

Mark Campbell,
Eagan, Minnesota

TV console gets new life as bookcase

I took this old TV stand and removed the TV and all of the parts, and I made it into a bookstand for my granddaughter.

The total cost for materials including stain and varnish was $90. I think it turned out really well.

Kedric Fairchild
Dendee, Michigan

Note from the Club:

Repurposing: *Projects (like Kedric's clever TV console conversion) that find a new use for an old item that has outlived its original function are of great interest to Club Members. Known as* repurposing *by some of us, this practice can be very rewarding and cost effective, as long as you keep a couple of basic rules in mind. First, avoid any repurposing projects that involve wiring unless you are an experienced electrical expert. And second, make sure any removed parts, like cathode tubes from a television, are disposed of properly—contact your local waste disposal agency for disposal information.*

Changing table doubles as chest of drawers

This is the changing table/chest of drawers that I designed and built for my new son. It is made of birch plywood panels with basswood trim and pine shelving for the drawer fronts. Its 52 in. length can be made more convenient for moving by removing six hidden screws and separating the high-boy from the chest.

The drawer fronts and tops are edged with a router and Roman Ogee bit, and the stiles are rounded-over. Because of the height of the top-most drawer (and the height of my 5 ft. 2 in. wife) I cut down the left drawer side for easier

accessibility. The design allows for use as a chest of drawers long after "changing" is over.

Larry Mann
Winterville, North Carolina

Open entertainment center

We were remodeling our house and were looking for a new entertainment center for our living room. My wife kept saying how big and closed-in all the ones we saw were. Our living room is not as big as we would like, and a big entertainment center would close it in more. I thought of building one out of manufactured cabinets, but this, too, would be overly big.

The design I created lets the wall show through behind it and all the glass shelves give it a light, airy feeling. It is painted in antique white, the same as our trim and doors, to help with the openness of the design. The carcase was assembled with ¾ in. particle board (since I was painting I didn't need high quality wood) and face molding for the column faces. The storage cabinets on the bottom were made with 1 × 2 pine for the face frames, stiles and rails. The door inserts are ¼ in. plywood. I added crown mold-

ing at the top to give it a more finished look. I also added recessed lights above each column area for a little accent lighting. With the glass shelves, the light shines all the way through.

For the shelves, I used ⅜ in.-thick glass. I dadoed-in a channel and inserted a shelf rail so the shelves would be adjustable. The TV shelf is the only one that is fixed, and it rests on 2½ in. rails for support.

All in all, this was a simple project with big results. The finished project is 8 ft. tall, and each of the three column areas is 3 ft. wide.

I feel this is a project that may solve the problem many of us handymen have: too small of a family room.

Rick P. Landwehr
Austin, Texas

Hope chests spring eternal

Forty-five years ago I made a cedar chest for my wife. We had three daughters who all would probably like to have it someday. Since you cannot divide a chest 3 ways, I decided to build one for each daughter. I also have two daughters-in-law and a granddaughter, so I built six chests total. I used about 300 board feet of cedar, and it took me three months to put them all together.

John Piatt
Perrysburg, Ohio

Custom wine rack could fit anywhere

I built this wine rack to fit into a special cabinet space in the basement. It has nine racks, each with nine slots, to hold a total of 81 bottles of wine.

I used knotty pine, but had some problems with warping. If I had to do it again, I'd cut all of the supports ⅛ in. longer on each end, build the box portion first and then cut the supports to fit.

For the bottle supports and ends I used five four-foot-long 1 × 4s and five four-foot-long 1 × 6s. I drilled the holes and then sawed down the middle of the boards, having measured from both ends so that the middle slot was in dead center. I used two six-foot-long 1 × 8s for the side boards and one six-foot-long 1 × 8 ripped into strips to hold the bottle racks.

This design could be altered to fit anywhere, or to be free-standing.

Wilbur C. Meier
Everett, Washington

Discarded cherry logs blossom into beautiful dressers

My wife and I had a used bedroom set, and after 10 years of marriage we decided it was time for a new set. We went shopping and discovered that the sets we liked would cost about $1,800. About that time *Shopsmith* was at the local mall, so I bought one of their machines thinking I could use it to build a bedroom set for less than the retail price.

One day soon after, I noticed loggers working just down the road from my house, so I stopped to see if they would sell me some logs. They told me that I could take anything from a certain pile

for free. These logs were not first quality, or were less than 8 ft. long, so the loggers wouldn't be using them. I took three cherry logs that were about 6½ ft. long. I also saved some money by having a friend of mine, who has a sawmill, saw the logs for me. I built two dressers from the wood. One (shown above) is 62½ × 18½ × 30 in. and the other is 44 × 18½ × 52 in.

Steven J. Evans
Holland Patent, New York

A bench for all reasons

This sturdy little bench can be a quick and simple pine project for a Boy Scout troop, or a fine woodworking design resulting in a highly crafted piece of oak or walnut furniture. It can be used as a step stool, a child's bench, a plant stand, or a low-end table.

To attach the sides to the cross beam, drill ⅜ in. holes to countersink 2½ in. deck screws. Make sure the pre-drilled holes in the sides completely allow screw threads to slip. Cover the holes with wooden plugs.

To attach the top, drill ⅜ in. countersink holes to allow 2½ in. deck screws to protrude ade-

quately into the top. A thin 12 in. long drill bit will be needed to finish this hole.

If you wish to change the dimensions, be sure the sides of the top do not extend beyond the feet or it will be tipsy.

Philip Doescher
La Crosse, Wisconsin

This glider stays put

My project was to build a glider rocker. It's all made from red oak. I ordered the arms, brass rockers, bearing and spindles from a retail outlet. I used 8½ in. roller bearing. The arms are pressure-bent curved chair arms.

The time and labor hours were many, but always enjoyable.

Theodore Dudash
Crown Point, Indiana

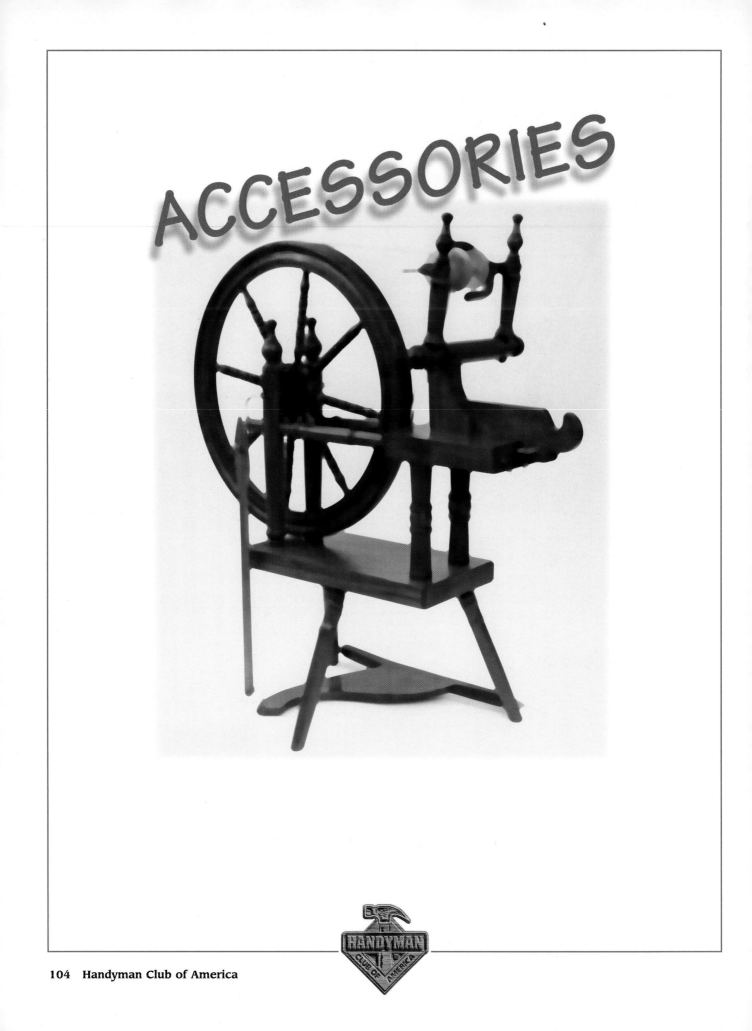

ACCESSORIES

Miniature Gazebo

I built this miniature gazebo by taking the original and miniaturizing it. The pictures and descriptions show how it was made.

Thomas Prejean
Sulphur, Louisiana

Miniature Gazebo: Step-by-step

Photo 1 The eight bottom frame pieces have 22½° miters and ¼ in. rabbets for the base. The width is 13½ in., and the top of the frame is chamfered. The 11½ in. posts are notched to fit the frames.

Photo 2 The top frame, made like the bottom frame, fits around the posts.

Photo 3 The roof-support post attaches to a framework in the top frame.

Photo 4 The roof beams span from the post to overhang the top frame

Photo 5 The rafters run from the top of the post to the beams at a 6-2 slope.

Photo 6 The 4 × 8 in. roof boards are laid edge to edge on the rafters, then pine trim and a cap are glued over the vertical seams.

A careful reproduction of an American Classic

This spinning (flax) wheel was constructed from American Walnut, cut from logs in Arkansas and air dried before I began working with it in my shop. This is the type of wheel that was commonly used (and still is in some remote areas) in the Midwest. It is essentially a wood-turning project. I had no patterns to work from, so I designed it myself.

William Marsella
Lynbrook, New York

Father Time

Here's a little project I just finished for a contest in Wisconsin. It's carved from a 2 × 10 pine plank. The inner circle of the time ring is sheet copper. A sheet copper door in the rear covers the battery cavity.

Charley Kimball
Drummond Island, Michigan

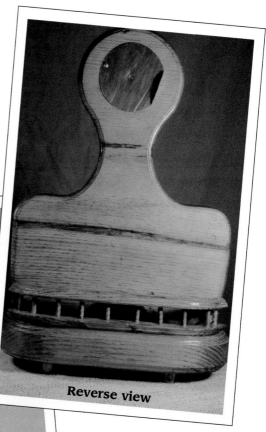

Reverse view

COLONIAL SPINNING WHEEL (oak)

WALKING WHEEL (oak)

Headstock modification helps master spinning wheel maker pursue his craft

Editor's Note: Club Member Earl Sorrels is a builder and restorer of spinning wheels—both full-sized working models and miniature versions. He turns most of the components himself on a mini wood lathe. Mounting small blanks and wood parts on the head stock is a real problem, but Earl came up with a clever solution.

One author of an instruction book I used said that once a spinning wheel bobbin is assembled and glued, it can't be put back in the lathe. That bugged me, until I made a modification to my little wood lathe. I simply drilled and tapped the headstock shaft to accept a 10 × 24, ³⁄₁₆ in.-dia. machine bolt. With the face plate installed, I can simply secure the workpiece with a ³⁄₁₆ in. nut. This enables me to make true turned items, faster and with repetitive accuracy. Anyone with a mini wood lathe can use this trick.

Earl Sorrels
Gig Harbor, Washington

NORWEGIAN SPINNING WHEEL
(black walnut)

Cutting grooves in a 9/16 in.-dia. flyer whorl mounted on a 10 × 24 machine screw in the headstock shaft.

Cutting drive band grooves on a 5 in.-dia. wheel for a miniature spinning wheel.

Cutting grooves in a bobbin whorl made for a full-size spinning wheel.

Changing times

This is a clock I made out of a piece of oak wood. I made it for my daughter and son-in-law the year they got their new home. The coins are that year: 1995. A silver dollar for 12 O'clock, a half-dollar for 6 O'clock, a quarter for 3 O'clock and 9 O'clock, and dimes for the rest. And it works well

DeLos Bohnsack
Dubuque, Iowa

Say it with wood

Over the years, I have enjoyed extending my creativity as an engineer to my amateur woodworking endeavors. I try to make everything in stock lumber sizes, often modifying plans or pictures accordingly, and have had some wonderful success. I also look to be the first at things, which always leaves a great impression.

So it was this past Valentine's Day when I decided to make (rather than buy) my wife's valentine. I cut two pieces of 1 × 8 to 10 in. long. I rounded over all the outside edges with a router, then routed hearts and a message of my choosing. I finished it with a honey stain and 2 coats of poly varnish, then painted the hearts red. She loves the gift and the thought. I loved the simplicity.

Ron Himmel
Hollidaysburg, Pennsylvania

Backyard lighthouse

This project was built to cover a water connection that protruded above the lawn. It is octagon shaped, 47 in. high and 19½ in. in diameter at the bottom.

All of the lumber used in this project was discarded as scrap by a local builder, and so it cost nothing. The bottom and top framework were made from 2 × 2 treated lumber. The sides were made from 1⅓₂″ pressure-treated exterior plywood. The corner strips were ripped from a 2 × 4, also pressure-treated, and were beveled 22.5° at the corners.

Base bricks were cut at the corners and set on-edge for ventilation. It is anchored by two pieces of 1½″ PVC pipe, and PVC tee fittings buried 10″ deep. The top platform was cut from a single piece of plywood. The railing was constructed from treated strips and golf tees that are mortised in, top and bottom.

The light enclosure was made from a clear flower pot, tier light diffuser, socket, and bulb. The steel roof was made from a cast-off light. Screws and epoxy were used throughout the project, and the inside corners are caulked. The platform is braced with quarter-round.

Herman C. Martin
Myrtle Beach, South Carolina

Rustic birdhouse

This unique birdhouse measures 12 × 12 in. and is divided in the middle to house two nests.

I used ¾ in. pine ripped down to ¾ × ¾ in. and end-dadoed, with all edges rounded to create a log effect. The door and window were then dadoed out. I finished it with ³⁄₁₆ in.-thick cedar trim.

The roof is made of ½ in. plywood and ⅛ in. cedar ripped down for shingles. The floor is ¾ in. plywood, screwed into the bottom to allow removal for cleaning.

Larry Hedtke
Franklin, Minnesota

Mini wishing well

This mini wishing well is built with #1 treated 1 × 6s and 2 × 4s, 2½ in. deck screws and corrugated fasteners. It has a shingled roof, a mini metal pail and a ¼ in. rope in a pulley. The only nails used are the roofing tacks. It takes seven 8 ft. 2 × 4s, one 8 ft. 1 × 6, eight shingles, 32 corrugated fasteners, 297 screws, four ³⁄₁₆ in. bolts and some roofing boards.

The well is 5 ft. high at the top, 24 in. in diameter across the base, and 17½ to 18 in. in diameter in the center of the well. The center well is made of split 2 × 4 pieces which are 12 in. long and cut at a 45° angle at the tips. It is eight rows high with the top row closed in.

I made this design with a pattern, and everything was done by judgment, instinct and desire. I have sold a few and am in the process of making more. Each one takes about 2½ days to put together. My wife took the first one I made and put an 18 in. plastic flower pot inside and is growing small flowers and vines in it—really pretty!

A.J. Schmitt
Midway, Georgia

Cherry mallet

I cut this mallet from a cherry log. All I needed was a dowel for the handle, a drill with a spade bit, and a bandsaw.

Phil Duck
Columbia, South Carolina

Keeping your thoughts in order

I believe that some of the best ideas one may ever have come shortly after going to bed and even in the middle of the night. It's a good idea to keep a hand-help tape recorder at the bedside for recording notes and memos. It's a good way to remind yourself to write them down the next morning.

Phil Duck

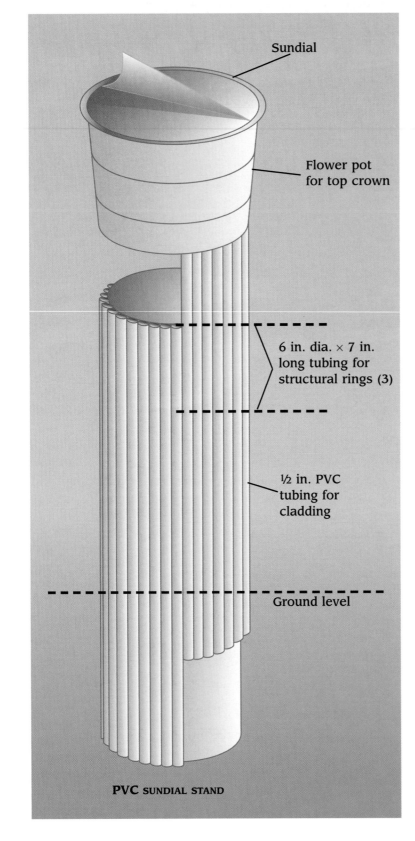

Sundial

Flower pot
for top crown

6 in. dia. × 7 in.
long tubing for
structural rings (3)

½ in. PVC
tubing for
cladding

Ground level

PVC SUNDIAL STAND

PVC sundial stand will pass the test of time

Two years ago I received a beautiful copper sundial as a gift. I searched everywhere for a suitable column to mount the sundial on, but could find nothing.

I decided to make one, so I checked with a local plumbing contractor and secured enough scrap pieces of ½ in. PVC pipe for my project. The core was made from a 21 in. long piece of 6 in. dia. PVC cut into three equal lengths for the top, center, and bottom. All other pieces, made of ½ in. PVC, were cut into 46 in. lengths and were fastened to the center pieces of 6 in. PVC with all-purpose drywall screws. All holes were drilled and countersunk. Once the assembly of 26 equally spaced tubes was finished, a little caulk took care of the rest—including covering the screw heads.

The top crown on the sundial stand was made from a flower pot with the bottom removed and the top reinforced, and the sundial was placed on the top. There is approximately 13 in. of column buried in the soil.

Herman C. Martin
Myrtle Beach, South Carolina

Bird feeder with a five-star rating

I designed this bird feeder for my sister-in-law in Charleston, South Carolina. I added a unique endurance feature to help the feeder withstand the elements: I slipped carefully hand-fitted square rings of wood over the main torso of the feeder. It's mounted in the rock garden in the back yard.

Phil Duck
Columbia, South Carolina

BACKYARD BUILDING

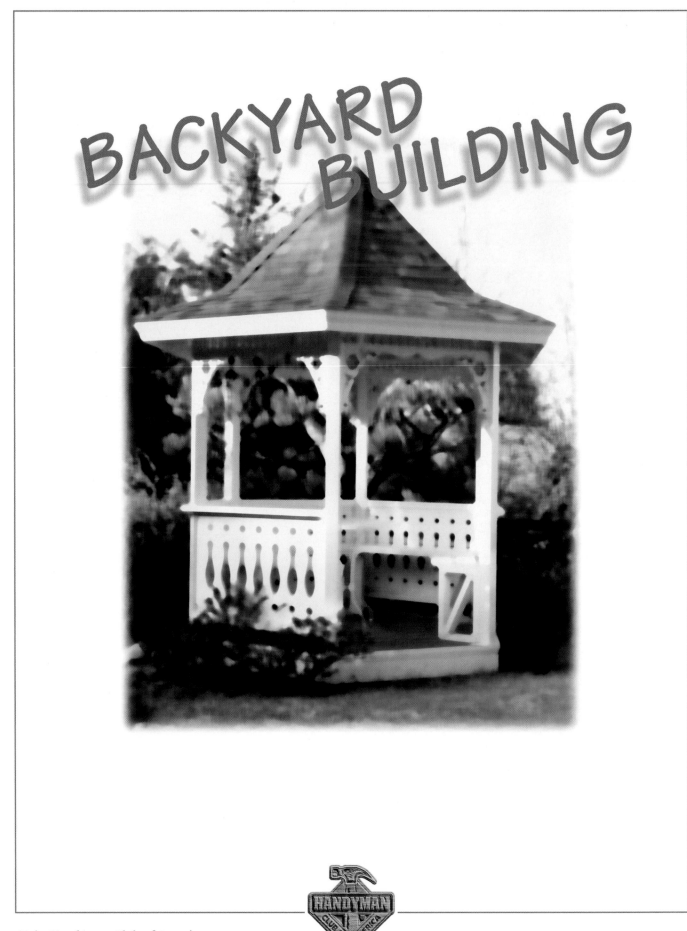

Swingers' Sanctuary

I constructed this two-person swing set entirely of native cedar, which I personally selected and harvested. The wood was allowed to cure for 4 to 6 weeks. All construction cutting was done with a chain saw—including the split side rails, which are used for drinks, food or utensils during a cookout. The swings are hung on hardwood dowels that pass through eye-bolts. The joints are secured with either bolts and nuts or all-thread rods with nuts, depending on the length required. These are invisible or only slightly visible.

The swing is set on a rock in a concrete base. My son has a similar swing at his house, which is set on grass.

Don Shaw
Opelika, Alabama

Wraparound barbecue area— formed and ready for finishing

I designed and built this patio barbecue area with a concrete block foundation and poured-in-place counter slabs that are reinforced and cantilevered. I installed a two-burner cooktop with twin gas grills, so chicken and beef don't have to be mixed.

The barbeque area also has a refrigerator and sink, arranged with the cooktop in a triangular configuration that is convenient for a cook and helper. There is plenty of space for bar stools around the countertop, and for storing supplies underneath the counter. The storage space is designed to accommodate a stereo system, as well as reverse-osmosis water purification system. A dishwasher could be built in if desired.

The cost of this project was low because concrete block and poured concrete are inexpensive building materials.

I plan to finish the countertop with Italian glass tile in a blend of four beautiful colors, and with stucco beneath the counters to match the house.

Bill Barnick
Poway, California

Wonderful water feature

This backyard patio project was done in our spare time by my wife, Helen, and myself, at very little cost, but with very rich rewards.

We started by tilling and removing dirt to level a back yard that was in total shade all day long—nothing but weeds ever grew there. We then used some spare bricks that were left over from bricking the house to border the flower beds that now line both sides of the patio.

We then picked up flagstone (common field stone) from around our small city lake and other places, such as along country roads, other lakes and rivers where we could find good, flat rocks. We used the field stone to form our patio, as my wife wanted a natural look to the entire project.

We then placed a working fountain with a turning water wheel on it at the center of the flower bed along the end of the patio on the side of the storage building. We placed a home-built picnic table on the patio. Finally, we placed some 50 or more tropical plants along each side in the flower bed areas, along the back flower bed area on either side of the water fountain, and in front of the fountain.

As you can see, it turned out great. We're very proud of it and now we spend a lot of time in the backyard. In summer, when the temperature is over 100°, it stays in the upper 80s on our beautiful patio. We love it, and hope you do also. It was hard work, but very rewarding.

Ray Adams
Hamilton, Texas

Open Sesame!

I was recently hired to put a deck on the rear of a 45-ft.-wide house. The house has a sliding glass door at one end, and a back door at the other. At the center of the house are two double-hung windows off the dining room. There is also a single double-hung near the back door for the kitchen.

This alone made for a standard deck with very little to set it off from others. But there was one problem that had to be dealt with: below the double-hung windows is the outside access door to the basement, with a set of steps leading down to the door. To maintain access without building a separate deck on either side of the basement door, I devised and constructed a set of doors that can be opened, but provide a flat,

sturdy deck when closed. To match the lines of the window, I built two doors (even though one door is the same width as the steps that lead down). To protect the access and prevent someone from falling, I hinged the hand rail and continued it across the opening. The skirting is also hinged so it can be opened.

The doors are 36 × 144 in., and weigh 250 pounds each. The joists for the doors were made of 2 × 6s with decking of 2 × 6 cedar. The weight of the doors raised concern that they would be unable to support several people at a party. To overcome this problem, I chiseled notches for 2 × 4s on the flat, and screwed and glued three 2 × 4 stiffeners under each door. To allow the doors to pass each other when opening or closing, I slanted the middle joist on each door 10 degrees. To raise and lower the doors, I mounted a boat winch assembly to the right side of the

opening. I attached cables to the doors by running them up the side and using pulleys mounted behind the header rails behind the top of the deck. When the doors are closed the cables are hooked along the vertical post at each side of the opening. Because of the winch, a single person can raise or lower the doors. For safety, when the doors are in the raised position there are gate catches attached to the vertical posts to hold the doors open.

While the doors and gates were a challenge to build, the real challenge was to put this all together so it looked good when closed. As you can see by the photos, all came together well.

Tommy G. Dudley
Kansas City, Kansas

Retractable deck conquers space/access challenge

I believe I have found a creative solution to a troublesome problem.

Our newly remodeled master bedroom was beautiful, but we thought it would be great to have a small private deck. Bordering the side of our house, however, is a convenience store, and in the back is our basement's hatchway. How could I build a deck over a hatchway? The answer was to hinge the section over the hatchway door.

The two old wooden hatchway doors were taken off and replaced with one that opens horizontally. The section of deck over the door was designed and hinged in the same direction. The lower section of lattice work was hung on eye hooks for easy removal. In case of an emergency, the door can be pushed up enough from inside the basement to make the lattice work pop off and allow an exit.

For those rare times when it is necessary to move large items to and from the basement, the deck section can be held up and out of the way.

Ron Puskas
Plantsville, Connecticut

Greenhouse on wheels

I recently built a portable greenhouse. It has three shelves measuring 3 × 4 feet for a total of 36 square feet of space for nursery plants.

The unit is mounted on two fixed and two swivel caster wheels, so it can be easily moved into a garage or another enclosure when the temperature is low enough to endanger plants. I also included a small, portable ceramic heater.

The framework consists of 2 × 4s with 2 × 2s on the doors in the front, back and top. The shelves are ½in.-dia. electrical thin-wall conduit,

providing good cross-ventilation. The screen-door hooks on the doors allow the doors to be closed or opened at various levels for ventilation. The whole unit is covered with reinforced greenhouse fabric, permitting good light penetration.

This greenhouse has easy access through the front, back and top, and its size and portability make it most useful. It will provide many years of service at minimal cost.

R. G. Hatfield
St. Paul, Nebraska

Glorious gazebo is setting for family memories

My husband, David, built this gazebo for our 25th wedding anniversary. We renewed our vows in it, and our daughter was married in it. David designed this gazebo himself, and it is our oasis of beauty in the desert.

Sherry A. French
for David G. French, Sr.
Tucson, Arizona

Note from the Club:

GAZEBOS: *A backyard gazebo seems to be on just about everyone's wish list—if they don't already have one. One of the reasons for the popularity of these whimsical structures is that they can be built in just about any size or style. The Victorian-style gazebo (two excellent examples are shown on these pages) has become the most popular and recognizable. But other traditional gazebos can look very different, sometimes sheathed in rustic twigs, bamboo, or even bedecked in ornamental wrought iron. But one feature all gazebos have in common is their geometric construction, consisting usually of five to eight symmetrical walls. If you're designing your own gazebo, the miter angles for cutting the perimeter boards depend on the number of walls. Here are the most common angles:*

Pentagon (5 sides): 36°
Hexagon (6 sides): 30°
Octagon (8 sides): 22½°

Solid redwood gazebo fulfills 45-year dream

My backyard building project was "inspired" by my wife of 48 years, who has spent 45 of those years wishing for a gazebo. I finally built it three years ago, and as a special favor for making her wait so long I built a companion grape arbor to replace our flimsy one.

I planned the gazebo board-by-board as I lay awake at night. I wanted a pleasing design of moderate size, in scale with our garden and our pocketbook. With much of the project made of redwood, keeping the cost within budget was as important as a beautiful design.

I chose a hexagonal shape for the gazebo for ease of calculation as well as appearance. The key to its construction was determining the location of the six vertical support posts. To assure accuracy in their placement, I determined the center of the floor and drove in a length of rebar as a pivot point. From old lath I made an equilateral triangle, the length of one side being half the distance between opposing posts. Placing the hole in the jig over the pivot, I located the approximate position of the first post, marking it with a stake. I then rotated the jig in five steps, staking each spot.

With a posthole digger I dug each hole about 20 in. deep and set my posts in loosely. Then I squared up the first post in exact position using supporting braces in two directions and checking with my jig many times. It took a bit of trial and error. When I was satisfied it was just right, I dumped in some dry posthole mix and some water until the level was an inch or so above the ground. I let it set overnight, then finished setting the rest in the same way, using my first post as a reference point. Once set, the tops were marked for level and cut off with a reciprocating saw, which is easy to do with redwood.

The rest of the construction was simple measuring, cutting and nailing. The floor is 2 × 6 redwood affixed to 2 × 8 redwood joists with galvanized deck screws. The seats and tops of the railing are 2 × 6 redwood, and the rest of the construction is pine.

I had never laid composition shingles, but found the process quite simple. I used half-inch plywood sheathing and roofing paper under them. I also added some lacework trim.

Ken Alexander
Lafayette, California

All-inclusive garden potting bench

My wife spends as much free time as possible working in the yard. Potting plants is one of her greatest pleasures, so she asked me to build a potting bench to allow her to easily perform her favorite tasks. Knowing that she has a bad back required that everything be at or above waist height, to keep her bending to a minimum. Easy access to tools, containers, water and soil preparations was also a necessity.

Using these criteria, I began my design. I researched several books and magazines and found articles which contained portions of what I wanted, and I incorporated them into my own all-inclusive plan. The simple design I came up with can be altered to suit most needs dictated by any site.

The basic frame is made from redwood 2 × 4s. The four uprights are cut to 7 ft. from standard 8 ft.

Top: The finished project boasts a tile potting surface, a wet sink with drainage, shelter from the sun, and ample ventilated storage enclosed by redwood lattice.

Left: A faucet carries water supply from the house and a drain hose connected to the sink leads to the garden.

stock. Two rectangular top/shelf support boxes are constructed of 2 × 4s to fit inside the uprights and maintain the 6 ft. × 27 in. overall bench dimension limits. One shelf support box is nailed in place about 6 in. from the ground to form the support for the inside lower storage shelf. The second top support box is nailed in place 3 ft. from the ground to provide the support for the bench top. Once the upper 2 × 4 bench top support box is installed, a 6 ft. × 27 in. piece of ¾ in. exterior plywood is cut and installed on the newly formed surface. Dado cuts are made in the four corners to accept the inset of the four uprights.

A 1 × 2 frame is placed around the perimeter of the plywood bench top, flush with the plywood top surface and overlapping the outside of the 2 × 4 uprights. This frame should be glued and nailed to the plywood edge. Near one end of the bench top a hole is cut in the plywood top for a plastic tub to be used as a sink.

Next, I installed 12-in. square tile on the bench top, then added a dark tobacco-colored grout after the tiles had set in the mortar base. The tile was allowed to set for a few days, then

The hinged lattice gates open to create access to the storage area. They were installed with a single cross rail that was cut after installation to ensure a perfect fit.

A close-up detail of the drain hose and how the connection is made to the sink drain.

the plastic sink was fitted with a drain and an adapter to allow connection of a garden hose remnant. The sink was set into a perimeter bead of RTV caulking.

The front enclosure doors are made from a single 6 ft.-long by 2½ ft.-wide 1 × 2 frame. I stapled redwood lattice to the door-frame assembly in two sections. I also attached lattice to each end of the enclosed bench area, and to the back of the lower bench area, extending about a foot above the bench top. A 6-ft. piece

of 1 × 2 along top edge of the one-foot-lattice overlap forms a trimmed edge.

Once this was done, I placed a 4 × 6 ft. piece of lattice on a 1 × 2 frame mounted on top of the 7 ft. vertical members to act as a sun-filtering shield above the potting bench. A 1 × 2 frame around the top lattice perimeter strengthens the lattice piece.

Finally, I ran a ½″ water line connected at the closest water source to a faucet in the potting bench and extended the drain hose out to the garden area. I set the structure on bricks to prevent ground contact, then applied redwood sealer to all wood surfaces.

John J. Adams
Newbury Park, California

Stylish gate adds interest to an ordinary deck

I designed and built this beautiful entrance gate for the deck on the back of my house. I made it from pressure-treated 2 × 2 pine. Eight years later, it still looks great!

Phil Duck
Columbia, South Carolina

Note from the Club:

Hanging gates: *Hanging a gate is a lot like hanging a door, but because the project is outdoors, most of us think of it as a rough carpentry task and sometimes we forget to plan. Swing direction, for example, is an extremely important consideration—especially if the gate is at the top of some stairs, like the one Phil has built here. Like doors, gates should always open toward the landing area, not toward the stairs. On level ground, try to hang gates so they open inward toward your yard (if you've ever been trapped in your yard by snow drifts from a blizzard you'll appreciate this).*

After

Before

River-rock walls increase curb appeal

We built two rock walls, and put boxwood plants between the walls, with red rock on the bottom next to the street. We moved the top plants around, and put in a sprinkler system. We also put rock around the birch tree on the left.

The rocks for the wall are river rocks from the Columbia River. My wife and I made many trips to the river.

Greg and Jamie Englert
Vancouver, Washington

Features:

- Dimensions: 30 in. deep × 60 in. wide × 69 in. high
- 846 sq. in. of primary cooking surface
- 330 sq. in. of chrome warming racks
- Two adjustable porcelain grills per section
- Porcelain-on-steel gas control panel
- Auto gas ignitor system with manual backup
- Thermometers in each lid
- Removable drip-pan/ashtray
- Storage box for utensils, etc.

The "ultimate" barbeque

I have designed and built the ultimate brick barbeque, featuring nearly 1200 square inches of cooking and warming surface.

The grill includes one section that cooks with propane and another section for charcoal cooking. I began the project by researching all the gas grills available. I bought the gas grill parts from a manufacturer. After carefully designing the brickwork to utilize these parts, the bricks were laid. I inserted steel to support the grills and the grates. Galvanized pipe was inserted to allow the stainless steel burners to be installed, and to create channels for the ignitor wires. Vent holes and a cast-iron cleanout door were also added.

Next, I formed sheet-metal grease/ash funnels for both sections. The lid supports were drilled, painted, anchored into the brickwork, caulked with heat-resistant compound, then grouted for a finished look. The modified gas control panel was attached to the brick with anchors. A metal base for the gas tank was made and attached to the grill with anchors. All metal parts were painted with a flat black paint to prevent rusting.

Finally the grill was trimmed with handmade, treated lumber chair rail, a tool storage box and two drop-down lids. Wooden pegs were added to allow the rosewood-handled cooking utensils to be displayed on the outside of the grill.

Don Moell
Fuquay-Varina, North Carolina

Plant-seeding device a real time-saver for serious gardeners

Editor's Note: For the true gardening enthusiast, Handyman Club Member Keith Huskey has devised a clever tool for uniform seeding of plant starter pots. Even if you don't do much gardening, we think you'll enjoy following along as Keith reveals the details of his innovative device.

Here is how my pneumatic seeder works. A one-gallon shop vac creates suction in a rectangular cube made of ¼ in.-thick *Plexiglass* (two strips of wood are placed inside the cube to prevent it from collapsing). Pin holes were drilled for seed spacing on the top surface, and a larger sized bit was used to funnel the holes slightly. The suction from the vacuum draws a single seed into each pin hole, while excess seeds roll into a side pocket when the seeder is rotated.

A pair of axel bolts inside a pair of brass bushings ensure smooth action when the seeder frame is rotated (the suction continues to hold the seeds in the pin holes).

This pneumatic seeder was very interesting to make and use for the first time this past spring. My cousin loaded the seeder and rotated it over while I placed the dirt-filled tray on the table. A small strip of wood is screwed into the tabletop to position the trays correctly under the seeder. I pushed the seeder down over the trays, then my cousin turned off the vacuum. The tray is perfectly seeded.

Keith Huskey
Dandridge, Tennessee

BUILDING PROJECTS

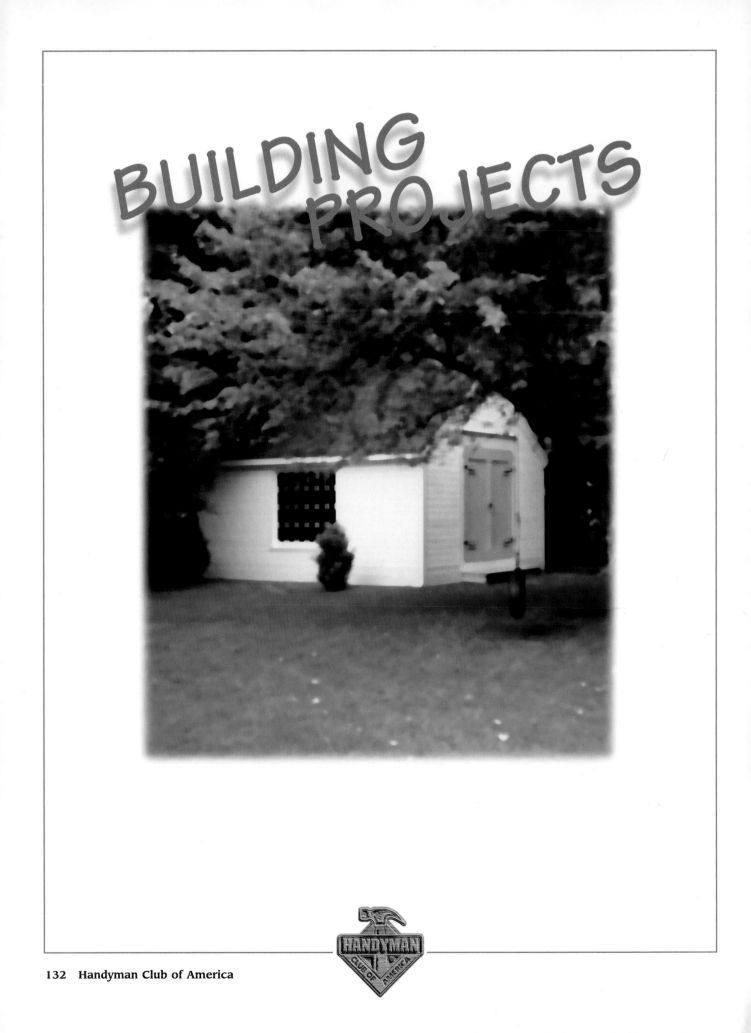

Mini-barn has big benefits

I needed some storage for lawn and garden equipment and seasonal patio furniture. After looking at kits I decided to create my own mini-barn, which fits right in here in Iowa.

The dimensions are 12 × 16 ft. with about 7 ft. of headroom on the main floor. The loft, accessible with a very sturdy one-piece ladder that pivots up into the ceiling, is 8 × 12 ft. with about 68 inches of headroom at the peak. The mini-barn sits on pre-molded concrete bases, each about 16 in. square, set on 4 ft. centers. The floor, and the 4 × 4s under the floor, are all made with treated lumber.

The stable-style doors provide access through the 75 × 78 in. front opening, with each of the four hinged units latching separately. I installed windows with screens on each side of the mini-barn. While the front loft "access" is only decorative, the small rear loft window is hinged to allow some ventilation.

My wife and I both love animals, so I built a little room underneath the mini-barn to provide rabbits, opossums, raccoons, etc. a shelter in the cold winter months.

Everything is on 16-in. centers and the roofing shingles are the 25-year type. Total cost of the project was about $2,650.

Steve Taylor
Muscatine, Iowa

Dutch Colonial styling turns shed into showpiece

When my relatives needed more room to store more garden tools, it became obvious that not just any ordinary shed would do. Their house is a 3,000-square-foot Dutch Colonial and we needed to match it as closely as possible. The shed also needed to be attractive enough to look at when sitting on the deck. We decided to build an 18 × 14 ft. shed with a 5 × 6 ft. picture window in front to give it real nice appeal with plenty of light inside.

Stefan Schumann
Meriden, Connecticut

A sure-fire trick for making double doors

Because the shed is oversized, it required an oversized door to match. I find that when making a double door, it's best to make the whole door in one piece first. I used 1 × 8 cedar boards to make the door, which should be ½ in. smaller than the size of the door opening. After assembling and squaring up the door, I installed a 1 × 8 border all the way around it. Then, I set the door in the opening, aligned it and shimmed it to leave a ¼ in. margin all around. I installed hinges on both sides of the door. I found the center of the door and made a level line down the door. With a circular saw, I cut the door in half. This made two doors that always make a perfect fit when the door is closed. After installing the lock set, I mounted boards on the insides of the two doors, from one corner to the other, so the doors would not sag.
~Stefan Schumann

State-of-the-art workshop nestled snugly into beautiful, rustic setting

My building project has been over two years in the making and includes a 30-foot lighted bridge and 500-square-foot workshop with bathroom, storage and porch. I designed it so that it could be easily converted into a studio apartment in the future. Except for a few hours assistance in lifting the sheathing onto the roof, I did all the construction myself with the help of a few scaffoldings and props to hold the roof joists in place.

The bridge is supported by 4 × 10 wood beams set on custom-made steel T-bar supports that are cemented into the river bank. The workshop sets on freestanding 6 × 6 posts sunk 36 in. into the soil, with 2 × 10 floor joists. Since I wanted to maximize the afternoon light, I gave the building a southwestern exposure with a full row of clerestory windows; for morning light, the east side of the roof incorporates a 4 × 6

With its lighted end posts, this wide footbridge provides convenient, friendly passage over the ravine abutting Mary's cozy, custom-built workshop.

An ambitious building project, this workshop boasts spacious work areas, plenty of natural light, and all the modern conveniences—even including cable TV service.

ft. skylight over the table saw and a 2 × 4 ft. skylight in the bathroom. I made all the windows and skylights myself from ¼ in. *Plexiglas* (which has proven to be a safe choice around the work areas), including two large picture windows and four sliders for ventilation.

The interior is finished in horizontal exterior hardboard siding painted white, with exposed joists and collar ties in pickled southern pine.

The exterior is natural, beveled cedar siding to match the main house. The building is fully insulated, has operational phone, cable TV, intercom, and heating and air conditioning. This past winter, the porch took on an unexpected use when it doubled as a dog nursery for my Labrador Retriever and her 10 puppies!

Mary Kenney
Durham, North Carolina

(Above) A small bump-out provides a dedicated, secure storage spot for gasoline cans.

(Left) The second floor of this shed houses two four-foot-high storage areas.

Two-story tool shed

My building project is a two-storey tool and storage shed. The floor is constructed of 10-ft. long pressure-treated 4 × 4s setting on 6 × 10 in. cement blocks (four blocks support each 4 × 4). The shed has five 12-ft.-long 2 × 4s on top of the 4 × 4s, with ⅝ in. tongue-and-groove plywood for a floor. The walls are constructed with standard studs and ⅝ in. exterior paneling, 4 in. on-center. The tallest part of the shed is 4 × 4 × 12 ft. It has two floors, with the second floor used for storing holiday decorations. The roof is galvanized metal. The shed also has a gasoline can holder attached to the outside of the back wall.

Glenn S. Sturgeon
Ceres, California

A single service door with barn-style cross rails provides easy passage into the side of this shed.

Log cabin styling gives rustic appeal to backyard shed

I recently completed a backyard storage shed that simulates the "square log" look of a log cabin. It has two windows and double doors in front, and it measures 12 × 20 ft.

I used rough lumber to frame the walls and roof. The painted metal roof has a 3 ft. overhang over the front double doors. I attached 4 × 8 sheets of ½ in. sheathing to all four sides of the shed. I then installed rough 2 × 6 oak planks horizontally, leaving a 3 in. space between each row, on top of the ½ in. plywood sheathing.

The 2 × 6 oak planks were painted using a custom mix earth-tone exterior latex paint. I filled the 3 in. spacing between each row of oak planks with a synthetic chinking compound used for chinking real log homes, just to give the project a bit more realism. I then cut, painted and installed 1 × 3 corner, window and door moldings.

The flower boxes under each window were made with rough 1 × 6 cedar. The floor and ramp were constructed with rough 1 × 6 oak planks.

All of the lumber used for this project was cut and dimensioned from 6 × 6 in. × 12 ft. air-dried rough oak, using a 24 in. band saw. The ½ in. plywood was purchased from the local lumber yard.

Ron McDowell
Gainesboro, Tennessee

STORAGE SOLUTIONS

Handy storage cubby created above basement door

I came up with a creative storage solution in our home. Our entryway has stairs going up to the living area, and stairs going down to the basement. The ceiling height from the top of the basement stairs was 12 feet. By lowering the ceiling above this landing, I was able to create a storage area with approximately 60 cubic feet of capacity.

I cut an access to this storage area into the wall above the basement stairs. This required partial removal of two wall studs. I followed this with some framing to rough out the opening, then installed a 1 × 4 frame and used clamshell trim for the finish.

I purchased two $10 shutters, cut them in half, and made doors out of them. We avoided the use of hardware on the outside by using push-to-open magnetic catches on the top and bottom of each door. The doors were painted white to match the living room.

Then I used 2 × 6 framing to create a floor in the area, which I secured to the surrounding framing with lag bolts. I installed cross members using joist hangers. The floor is covered with ¾ in. plywood, which had to be cut in half to fit through the opening. On the underside, ½ in. sheetrock, spackled and painted, created a nice finish. I did have to tweak the installation a bit, as I was unable to find even one square corner on the existing framing and walls.

The only power tools I used were a circular saw, a reciprocating saw, and a drill. I used a variety of hand tools, including an old-fashioned manual miter box for the trim.

The area is intended for long-term-storage, as you must use a ladder to access it. Let me tell you, that since our little girl was born, this space has been invaluable!

Michal Hofkin
Philadelphia, Pennsylvania

The two shutter doors above the basement door provide access to a space-efficient storage area framed in an area that formerly was excess ceiling space above the landing to the basement stairs.

Under-stairs entertainment center

Originally the space below my stairs was strictly a closet area. After many years of using a traditional TV stand, I came up with the idea of building a built-in entertainment unit, including a closet. This idea has become a great success and it has increased our living space by at least one square yard. It also modernized our living room appearance.

Inside the entertainment unit are all the outlets needed for electrical, stereo and cable TV use. No wires are exposed from the electronic components. Many friends and family have complimented this original space-saving project.

Sal Salvia
Roscoe, New York

Efficient stock-holder provides dividends

An old floor style lamp post and a few coffee cans (some open on both ends) make an excellent space-saver and organizer for long, thin stock. The cans are riveted to the post top and bottom.

Richard G. Ernst
Phoenix, Arizona

Top-notch trick for storing topper

I recently bought a truck with a camper shell. I needed a quick and inexpensive way to remove the shell and keep it protected from the weather.

I cut 2 × 4s approximately 5 in. taller than the bed of my truck. Then I cut a notch in the top of each 2 × 4 to accept another 2 × 4 on-end. I nailed two 2 × 4s onto the wall in my single car garage 6 ft. apart on one side of my garage, and nailed the other two onto the other wall opposite the first ones. Then I measured the distance between the two opposite walls and cut a 2 × 4 to connect the two walls together. This built a simple removable frame to store my shell on.

Now when I want to take my shell off, I back my truck into the garage. I unbolt the shell, lift the back end, and slide the long 2 × 4 runner under the shell to the front braces. Then I lift the back of the shell and slide the second long 2 × 4 runner under the shell to the front braces. I lift the shell high enough to set the 2 × 4s in the slots on both ends. Then I attach the shell clamps back on the shell on each side of the 2 × 4s to prevent the shell from being shoved forward or backward.

Now all I have to do is drive the truck out from underneath the shell. The shell is now stored in the garage, and ready and waiting to be put back on.

Joint detail

I can remove or install the shell in only 15 minutes by myself. The setup materials included four 10-ft. 2 × 4s and a few nails or screws, and can be built with just a hammer, measuring tape and hand saw.

William G. Waldram
Topeka, Kansas

Rack keeps firewood organized and off the ground

You can utilize the outside of your shed as well as the inside. I built a shelf for storing firewood on an outside wall of my shed. This keeps the wood off the ground and dry until I'm ready to use it.

Chuck Woolley
Kokomo, Indiana

Note from the Club:

STORING FIREWOOD: *Firewood can create some challenging storage problems. In many cases, there are municipal codes governing the amount of wood you can store in your yard, as well as acceptable locations for the wood pile. For example, many communities will not allow you to store firewood in the front of your home. Check with your local building and safety department to learn about any applicable codes before you spend time and money creating a firewood storage area.*

Small closet makeover

In a mountain cabin or small home, space is at a premium for convenient storage. You need places to put cookie sheets, baking dishes, serving trays, platter, barbecue set, canned goods, staples, extra paper goods, as well as brooms, feather duster, dust mop, dustpan, ceiling fan brush, fly swatter and toilet plunger.

After some remodeling in our cabin, I ended up with a 28 × 30 × 86 in. closet. With some careful thought, my wife and I designed the innards for maximum use as a pantry next to the kitchen.

The drawer cabinet is made from particle board and tempered hardboard, attached direectly to the ceiling of the closet. The drawers are made from drawer kits. The wire racks are pruchased in prefabricated form.

The project probably could be completed in about two days, if our vacation days were just devoted to completing this project. The total cost was about $135.

Gene Smith
Whittier, California

REMODELING SUCCESSES

Inspiration calling...

My remodeling project is a closet that I turned into a phone booth. To accomplish it, I removed all items, took down the closet rack and installed a light in the ceiling, including a switch. Then I removed the louvers from the top half of the bifold doors and installed plate glass that I hand painted. I had to install quarter-round in the opening of the bifold to hold the glass in place.

Next I hung wallpaper down to the wainscot paneling that I painted *Coca-Cola* red. I then installed a pay phone that I had owned for 18 years, and bought a red stool.

Vincent J. Falini III
Dunedin, Florida

Before

Split-log facelift

The most unique thing about this remodeling project is that all of the lumber I used on the outside of this building was purchased from a sawmill in rough form. I let these 6 × 6 in. × 12 ft. beams air dry for nine months before using them.

I used this lumber to remodel the outside of my 24 × 44 ft. woodworking shop, which was previously sided with *T111* siding and had no decks or overhangs over the front and side doors.

The new log siding, which I made in my shop, is 1½ in. × 5½ in. Here in Tennessee there are many sawmills where you can purchase rough lumber of many different types. By using a bandsaw and shaper I was able to mill this beautiful log siding. I custom-made the railing and spindles that enclose the front and side of the building. The top of the railing is actually a piece of the log siding with the lip and tongue cut from both sides to make a 4½ in. cap along

the top of the rail, so rainwater will not collect on top of the rail.

The front and side decks were made from rough oak, which I dimensioned to 1 × 6 in. × 12 ft. planks. The front double-hung doors were sided, with the log siding installed in a vertical position. I also closed in the bottom of the front and side deck using the log siding in the vertical position.

The roof of the building consists of 3 ft.-wide metal panels that overlap each other to form a water-tight roofing system. These panels are available in an assortment of colors.

The side of the building has a single garage door and loading area where I can back up my truck to load or unload materials.

All of the exterior wood was stained with a custom-mixed oil-based stain containing linseed oil, tung oils, *UV* blockers and mildew-resistant inhibitors.

Ron McDowell
Gainesboro, Tennessee

"Pocket" screen door

To increase ventilation, I built a sliding screen door in the entry from the garage to the house. It keeps insects and other critters from entering the house while letting fresh air into the home. A sliding door uses less space and is less obtrusive than a regular swinging door. This door slides behind a freezer in our garage.

We affixed a wood frame to the garage side of the wall, which extends beyond the doorway, to allow the slider to clear the doorway. The frame is constructed of 2 × 3 wood. The slider travels on a ½ in. L-shaped aluminum rail, and the top of the door travels in a 1 in. U-shaped aluminum track. On each side the door slides into a U-shaped track, providing a seal when the door is closed.

Richard W. Green
Thousand Oaks, California

Country kitchen

Our home is 20 years old. The kitchen cupboards were pressboard, the counters were rolled vinyl, and the floor was press-on tile. The roof leaked and the ceiling caved in over the kitchen sink.

My husband, David, remodeled the kitchen using pine and glass to show off my antique dishes. The light is of his own design, to cover the ceiling cave-in. The rolling island is made of butcher block, with storage space for pots and

pans. It also includes a knife drawer he designed. The counters are covered with ceramic tile. *(Editor's Note: For another view of David's built-in hutch, see page 94 in the* Furniture Projects *section).*

Sherry A. French
for David G. French, Sr.
Tucson, Arizona

Before

Victorian kitchen

The kitchen in our 1880s Victorian home had been remodeled in 1974 by the previous owner. The L-shaped kitchen was only 8-ft. wide and had no windows in the wing where the cooking center was located. It had dark stained cabinets, a suspended ceiling, and boxed-in soffits.

To brighten and modernize the kitchen without spending a lot of money, we chose to paint the cabinets white (inside and out), remove the suspended ceiling and soffits and put the ceiling back to its original 9 ft. height.

I removed the old plaster from the original ceiling, shimmed the ceiling, rewired, insulated and installed drywall. Then I designed a ceiling treatment that was based on 4 ft. square blocks

of beaded board paneling that used poplar boards in a grid. The edges of the boards were rabbeted ¼ in. deep on the back to accommodate the paneling, and a ½ in. ogee on each face edge softened the appearance. Where the boards intersected, the ends were machined to

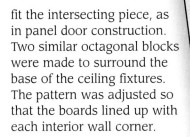

fit the intersecting piece, as in panel door construction. Two similar octagonal blocks were made to surround the base of the ceiling fixtures. The pattern was adjusted so that the boards lined up with each interior wall corner.

Two open shelf cabinet units were built to extend the cabinets to the end of one wall, and the countertop was also extended. The original laminate was removed and new laminate installed. A new sink and faucet were also installed. The dark vinyl floor was replaced with white polyurethane-surfaced floor tile.

Wallpaper with a dusty rose motif, rose dust countertop material, and ceramic tiles with roses accent the wall protection behind the stove. There is a pass-through to the dining room, which is finished in deep burgundy. The burgundy appears in designs on the white floor tile, while the rose colors repeat the reddish tones.

Two Victorian-style light fixtures were chosen for general lighting: a five-globe suspended unit and a sister three-arm unit in the cooking center aisle. Seven recessed ceiling lights provide concentrated light over the countertops and at the outside entry area. Dimmer switches are on all circuits.

The total cost was under $2,600. It took approximately 180 hours over five months to complete the project. We now have a much brighter kitchen that appears roomier because of the increased vertical space and the extra width over the top of the cabinets. The ceiling treatment gives visual interest and vertical texture.

Martin G. Sierk
Warsaw, New York

In addition to providing plentiful storage and giving the basement a customized apperance, this builtin floor-to-ceiling bookcase successfully hides an elevated waste line behind the two center panels at floor level.

Re-do transforms dark basement into pleasant family room

When my wife and I moved into our house four years ago, we both got what we wanted. She got a dining room and I got a den. I'm a musician, and I have a lot of equipment. I needed a clean, dry room where I could practice and keep my gear. A room in our basement was just that. But it had dark paneling, poor lighting, and it didn't make great use of its space.

About seven months ago, I noticed in some places we were getting more and more mildew, and that some of the paneling was peeling away from itself ply-by-ply. I figured moisture was starting to seep through the walls, and I should do something sooner than later. I also needed more space. I have a two-year-old, and he needed a place for his toys, too. So, I decided to gut and redesign the room.

I took the room back down to cinder block and found I was right: there was a seepage problem. I scraped off the loose material with a wire brush and a pry bar in some cases, and gave it a good washing. I patched the holes and painted the room with moisture-sealing paint. Next, I put up ¾" polystyrene insulation all around the room, attaching it with construction adhesive, and put duct tape over each seam. Then, I put up furring strips with a powder-actuated stud gun and covered the whole thing with a 6-mil poly vapor barrier.

I had an electrician do the rough-in for some additional outlets, and I put in a separate phone line for our computer. I also took the liberty of running speaker wire behind the drywall, which was followed with paint, wainscoting, and crown molding. All the ceiling needed was a coat of paint and a little patching.

While I was at it, I found a floor padding made of heavy foam rubber about ¾" thick. It came in 4 × 4 ft. sections that went together like a puzzle. It was recommended for workshops, playrooms and gyms. It makes a huge difference in the comfort level.

Now came the big project. Along the back wall of the room, I had an obstacle where the waste line to the street was elevated. I decided to design and build a bookcase that would go around the waste line and span the entire wall, allowing for more storage.

The two bottom shelves are for my son's toys and are a good height for a toddler. The panels on the bottom conceal the waste pipe, but are hinged to provide access. To the far left is a drawer for storage, and the double doors above that are actually one door that folds down as a secretary-style desk, and conceals our computer. The phone line for faxing and the electrical outlet are built right in. The whole thing is made out of ¾ in. luaun veneered plywood. I got the fluted columns at the home center, and bought embossed moldings and carvings to dress it up, along with some hardware, from a woodworking supply catalogue.

Ray Jandura
Clifton, New Jersey

Previously hidden by old paneling, the walls in this basement area allowed some water seepage (top). A coat of moisture-sealing paint helped alleviate the problem (bottom).

Cheerful colors and light-toned wainscoting helped make this basement remodeling project a success story.

A custom-made bay window is the centerpiece of this remodeling project that transformed a garage into a spacious and comfortable master bedroom.

Garage becomes a master bedroom

Recently, I converted a 12 × 22 ft. garage into a master bedroom, full bath, and walk-in closet. All framing, wiring, plumbing, dry walling and woodwork was done by myself in my spare time. The highlight of this project was designing and constructing the bay window from two 25 × 56 in. end windows and a 41 × 56 in. center window. I added a built-in cedar chest in the window base.

Lance Mack
Eau Claire, Michigan

The custom bay window was fashioned from three double-hung window units. The seat board doubles as a lid for a cedar chest.

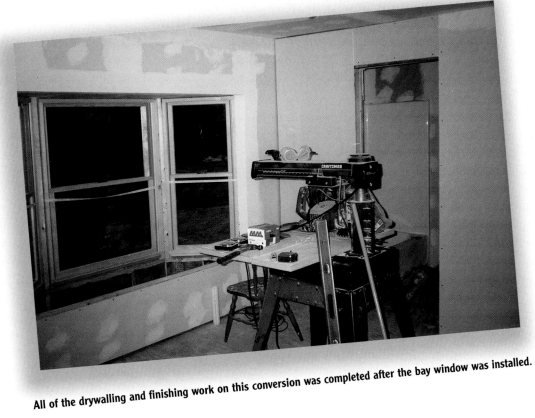

All of the drywalling and finishing work on this conversion was completed after the bay window was installed.

Index